SUDAN

SUDAN

STATE AND SOCIETY
IN CRISIS

EDITED BY

John O. Voll

Indiana University Press
Bloomington and Indianapolis

Published in association with
the Middle East Institute
Washington, DC

The following chapters appeared previously in *The Middle East Journal*, Volume 44 (No. 4, Autumn 1990): Peter K. Bechtold, "More Turbulence in Sudan: A New Politics This Time?"; Francis Mading Deng, "War Visions for the Nation"; Carolyn Fluehr-Lobban, "Islamization in Sudan: A Critical Assessment"; Gabriel R. Warburg, "The *Sharia* in Sudan: Implementation and Repercussions"; Mary C. Kilgour, "Refugees and Development: Dissonance in Sudan"; and Stephen Kontos, "Farmers and the Failure of Agribusiness in Sudan."

The paper used in this publication meets the minimum requirements of American National Standard for Information Sciences—Permanence of Paper for Printed Library Materials, ANSI Z39.48-1984.

Manufactured in the United States of America

Library of Congress Cataloging-in-Publication Data

Sudan : state and society in crisis / edited by John O. Voll.
    p.   cm.
    Includes index.
    ISBN 0-253-36270-9 (cloth).—ISBN 0-253-20683-9 (paper)
    1. Sudan—Politics and government—1956–   I. Voll, John Obert,
date. II. Middle East Institute (Washington, D.C.)
    DT157.3.S84   1991
    962.404—dc20   91-13026

1   2   3   4   5   95   94   93   92   91

Contents

Preface

The June 30, 1989, military coup in Sudan is part of the growing crisis of state and society in that country. The Sudanese face civil war, famine, growing numbers of refugees, major economic difficulties, and political instability. These grave problems, however, have not always dominated Sudanese affairs. In the past four decades there have been many times when optimistic assessments of conditions in Sudan have been possible. This volume examines a number of critical dimensions of the contemporary Sudanese experience in an effort to understand how the current situation has developed and how solutions may be found.

The potential strengths of society and state in Sudan require that one not concentrate solely on crises and problems. Sudan has, at various times, been seen as a possible model for parliamentary democracy, an example of interethnic cooperation in the African context, and a potential "breadbasket" for its region and continent. Sudan possesses land and water resources appropriate for agricultural development, newly discovered oil reserves, a cosmopolitan educated class, and political organizations that successfully bridged the gap between the more "traditional" elements and "modern" groups in society.

Specific events and developments show this positive potential. The October Revolution of 1964 revealed the latent strength of the democratic tradition—it was one of few instances when mostly unarmed civilians were able to overthrow a military regime and replace it with a democratically elected parliament. This experience was repeated, in somewhat different ways, in 1985–1986. The potential for interethnic cooperation is shown in the agreement reached in 1972 that brought an end to 17 years of civil war. This agreement was hailed by many as an example of how national unity could be created on the basis of recognition of shared diversity. The economic potential of Sudan was recognized, especially in the mid-1970s, with large-scale international investment in Sudanese agricultural projects.

The tragedy of Sudan is that all these positive factors have been matched by negative ones. The threat of violent interethnic conflict seems increasingly to be realized, not just in the resumption of the civil war in 1983 but also in the number of smaller conflicts that have reached highly destructive levels, especially in the western rural areas. The economy has collapsed, and the country faces the grave problems of a debtor nation in decline. Growing numbers of people are being uprooted by the conflicts, and refugees have become a significant element in Sudanese society. The third era of civilian parliamentary rule came to an end in the 1989 coup, and Sudan is ruled now by a controversial, military-dominated government. In this context of crisis, people now speak of the possibility of Sudan becoming "another Lebanon" and deteriorating into social, economic, and political anarchy.

Peter Bechtold provides an analysis of the basic political dynamics of modern Sudan in his contribution to this volume. The alternation between parliamentary and military regimes raises the question of why both types of government have failed. The special style of factionalism that has been characteristic of Sudanese politics continues to be an important negative force. Neither civilian party politics nor military revolutionary programs have been able to overcome the basic factors of instability in the country.

Factionalism and divisions underlie the tensions within Sudan, and Francis Mading Deng reminds us in his chapter that diversity need not necessarily lead to open conflict. Pluralism can provide resources for a special national identity. In the past there were hopes that Sudan might be an Afro-Arab microcosm that could constructively link Africa and the Middle East in sociocultural affairs. The current crisis in Sudan involves a "war of visions" for the Sudanese nation. Deng believes that the main ideals for effective national unity are accepted by most Sudanese, but that many difficult compromises will be necessary for the achievement of that unity.

Domestic instability has an important impact on Sudan's role in international relations. Ann Mosely Lesch examines the complex relationships between domestic politics and international conditions. In this context, the potential for positive developments tends to be over-ridden by the impact of the overwhelming problems of Sudanese po-litical instability and economic difficulties.

The search for a unifying principle leads many northern Sudanese leaders to advocate basing the political system in some way on Islam. Carolyn Fluehr-Lobban examines how Islamization efforts arouse fears and tensions that have historical roots in Sudan. While Islam may pro-vide a basis for some form of unity in the northern regions of the country, Islamization of the nation-state creates divisions between Muslims and non-Muslims, and also—among Muslims themselves—between Islamists and those with a more secularist perspective.

The "September Laws" promulgated by Jaafar al-Numayri in 1983 represent a critical turning point in the history of Islamization in Sudan. Fluehr-Lobban looks at Numayri's Islamization in the historical con-text of problems of national unity. Gabriel Warburg provides an ex-amination of the political and intellectual development of "the Islamic Path" as a basis for policy under Numayri. Warburg then shows why it was impossible, after Numayri was overthrown in 1985, for even political opponents of the September Laws to repeal them in the era of parliamentary politics in the 1980s. The effective political power of the Muslim Brotherhood is an important element in this situation.

The Sudanese face staggering economic and social problems that strengthen the forces of instability and are, in important ways, products of that instability. Bodour Abu Affan describes some of the basic pat-terns of the economic problems and examines the attempt to implement a stabilization program at the end of the 1970s. The failure of this program may indicate both the intractable nature of Sudanese eco-nomic problems and the ineffectiveness of the standard approaches to the economic crises of countries like Sudan.

Mary C. Kilgour demonstrates the magnitude of the refugee problem in Sudan and the way in which it affects economic developments in general. Large numbers of refugees have fled to Sudan from the fighting and famine in Ethiopia and Chad, adding to the already difficult prob-lem of internally displaced Sudanese. Kilgour notes that in 1988 alone, "250,000 people died of war-related famine and disease." Kilgour ex-

plains the institutional and organizational obstacles to providing effective relief for refugees. Long-term planning and development
projects are made virtually impossible by limitations on the donors and
by the attitudes of the Sudanese government and opposition. United
States development aid is currently restricted by legislative provisions
that Kilgour suggests might, for humanitarian reasons, be reviewed.

Prospects for resolving issues of national unity depend to a significant degree on the strength of the Sudanese economy. Although there
has been some industrial development, the agricultural sector remains
in many ways the key to a healthy Sudanese economy. Stephen Kontos
notes that despite the investment of billions of dollars in Sudanese
agriculture between 1975 and 1985, large-scale commercial agriculture
has not been successful and has, in fact, helped to create the current
grave debt problems in Sudan. The huge and longstanding Gezira
scheme faces major problems, and other more recent schemes have
failed. Kontos suggests the importance of reversing the trend toward
greater government control and centralization in Sudanese agriculture
and providing in its stead more freedom, incentives, and support for
small farmers.

The stark realities of current conditions represent a crisis of major
proportions for state and society in Sudan. The essays in this volume
make clear the magnitude of the crises and show that there are no
simple solutions. The relationships between the different aspects of the
current situation create a vicious circle that is difficult to break. It
appears that political instability will continue as long as governments
are unable to resolve the major economic problems of the country, yet
resolution of those problems requires a relatively high level of political
stability in order to encourage investor and farmer confidence. Most
Sudanese recognize the necessity of having a political system in which
all Sudanese can participate with a sense of equality and national unity,
yet the most thoroughly articulated visions of a "national identity"
tend to be *exclusive* rather than encouraging an *inclusive* sense of what
it means to be "Sudanese."

It is essential that the discussions of Sudan and its prospects not stop
with a simple assessment of blame. Islamists and secularists, northerners and southerners, people from all of the different and diverse

groups within Sudan and their friends outside Sudan cannot resolve Sudan's problems by accusing someone else. Sudan needs all of these people to begin developing ways to work together constructively. The past has shown that overthrowing the existing government, whatever the nature of that government, has not caused any of the fundamental problems of disunity or economic difficulty to disappear. The authors of the essays in this volume identify the problems and suggest potential lines for resolving them.

The alternatives facing the Sudanese in the present crisis are stark. Francis Deng puts the issue clearly when he notes that the question for Sudan is one of "making history in a positive sense or being a victim of history."

I want to express my appreciation for all the help that I have received in the preparation of this volume from Jean C. Newsom, whose guidance made possible the publication of the special issue of the *Middle East Journal* on which it is based. Thanks are also due to Joan Kontos for her special editorial help.

John O. Voll

SUDAN

More Turbulence in Sudan

A NEW POLITICS THIS TIME?

Peter K. Bechtold

The Republic of Sudan is an extraordinary country in the true meaning of the term. The largest country in Africa and the Middle East—with just under 1 million square miles of territory—Sudan straddles both of these cultural and geographic regions. Its 597 tribes speak more than 400 languages and dialects and practice a variety of religious traditions within each of three major groupings: Islam, indigenous African beliefs, and Christianity, in that quantitative order. Moreover, the combination of Hamitic, Semitic, Nilotic, Bantu, and other ethnic groupings has resulted in one of the world's most heterogeneous societies that is almost a microcosm of Africa.

Sudan's size and diversity—both in land and in population—provide an extraordinary challenge to any government. When one considers the additional characteristic of the country's strong and genuinely democratic political culture, it is easy to understand why political stability has been difficult to achieve there. Indeed, during the past five years Sudan has had four distinct governments ranging from the Jaafar al-Numayri military dictatorship that fell in April 1985, through a year-long transitional regime under a mixed civilian and military leadership, several coalition governments during the parliamentary rule of Prime Minister Sadiq al-Mahdi, to the June 30, 1989, assumption of power by a junta led by Umar Hassan Ahmad al-Bashir (then colonel, now lieutenant general, and henceforth referred to here as Bashir).

At least three additional factors make Sudan an extraordinary country. Its particular racial, ethnic, and religious mix has posed enormous challenges for Sudan's identity, ranging from its being a bridge between the Arab and African worlds in happier times, to political conflict and outright civil war in others. It is also one of the few Third World nations with considerable economic potential, especially considering its abundance of water and arable land, and has been identified as a potential "food basket" by several international organizations, notwithstanding the terrible current condition of the Sudanese economy.[1] Finally, on not one but two separate occasions, long years of military rule were ended by popular uprisings when an unarmed populace forced juntas out of office with virtually no violence or bloodshed.[2]

There are at least two schools of thought about the Bashir government and its likely staying power. One school offers a basically cyclical analysis in that all military regimes in Sudan have come about as a result of shortcomings of civilian parliamentary governments and will last only until a sufficiently large segment of the body politic coalesces to dispose of them and returns democratic rule. The other approach looks for fundamental changes in the sociopolitical order and views recent coup attempts—including the successful one of June 1989—not merely as political alternatives, but as evidence of a more basic transformation of the entire system—a change from "old politics" to "new politics," as it were. This article presents a third alternative, arguing for a combination of both perspectives, symbolized by the official name that the junta has chosen for itself—the Revolutionary Command Council of National Salvation (RCC-NS)—signifying an alternative to civilian mismanagement, but with a definite ideology. This ideological dimension differentiates the new government from previous military regimes, but, to understand this orientation and its implications for regime policy and stability, a comparative context to the predecessor governments is needed.

From Independence to National Salvation

Since Sudan obtained independence from the Anglo-Egyptian Condominium on January 1, 1956, its governments have oscillated between

Westminster-style parliamentary democracy and military rule. Independence itself resulted from an act of the Constituent Assembly, freely and fairly elected in 1953 by any reasonable standard, as have all successive parliaments in contrast to most others in the Arab world and Africa.[3] The first democratic government was led by Prime Minister Ismail al-Azhari of the National Unionist Party until July 1956 and was followed by another under his Umma Party rival, Abdallah Khalil. Frustrations over inter- and intra-party maneuvering plus frequent legal and illegal strikes induced Khalil in November 1958 to ask General Ibrahim Abbud, his former schoolmate and then armed forces chief of staff, to assume power until such time as "the mess could be straightened out, stable economic conditions would come about, and the army would return to its barracks."[4]

Immediately after the change in government on 17 November, political parties and strikes were quickly outlawed, and the country was ruled by the Supreme Council of the Armed Forces under Abbud's chairmanship. The economic decline under civilian rule was reversed. In a remarkably brief period, Sudan acquired both political and economic stability except for a lingering rebellion in the south, which had erupted under the Azhari administration in August 1955.[5] Instead of returning to the barracks, as promised, the junta remained in office for almost six years until it was finally pressured to resign by an unarmed civilian uprising on October 21, 1964. This event has assumed considerable significance in the modern political history of Sudan and is still revered as the "October Revolution." October 1964 brought two important new forces with new ideas onto the country's political scene: an alliance of professionals disenchanted with the influence of traditional tribal and sectarian leaders and the public emergence of noncentrist movements—the Muslim Brotherhood, whose political organization then called itself the Islamic Charter Front, and the Communist Party of Sudan.

After a transitional period of six months, general elections were held in areas unaffected by the civil war in the south, and parliamentary rule returned in May 1965. Four years and several coalition governments later, the political, economic, and security conditions resembled those of autumn 1958, before the Abbud takeover, and public confidence in liberal democracy sank to a comparable low. Colonel Jaafar

MAP OF THE SUDAN

Source: Reprinted by permission of Greenwood Publishing Group, Inc., West-
port, CT, from *Politics in the Sudan: Parliamentary and Military Rule in an
Emerging African Nation,* by Peter K. Bechtold. Copyright © 1976 by Praeger
Publishers, Inc., New York, NY.

al-Numayri and some junior military colleagues aligned themselves with the mostly leftist professionals from the October 1964 revolution and seized power on May 25, 1969.

Once again, all political parties were outlawed, their leaders imprisoned, and a revolutionary command council was set up to govern the country. The regime referred to itself as the May Revolution, called for a return of the principles of the October Revolution, and promised a new order not based on the traditional centers of power. Even though generally unpopular at home—except for a brief period in the early 1970s—Numayri and his regime surprised many by surviving almost 24 coup plots and actual attempts until April 6, 1985, when the armed forces commander in chief, Lieutenant General Abd al-Rahman Siwar al-Dhahab, took control of the country and deposed Numayri who was returning from a state visit to Washington.

The next 50 months almost duplicated the period of October 1964 to May 1969: first, a transitional period leading to general elections in April 1986 in those areas unaffected by a new rebellion in the south; then, a series of coalition governments all characterized by political stagnation, economic decline, and a further deterioration of the security situation in the face of rebellion. There were also some new elements: major droughts previously unheard of; the worst unseasonal flooding in the Khartoum area in more than a hundred years; and the debilitating effects of a foreign debt—mostly accumulated during the Numayri period—so huge that it exceeded Sudan's annual gross domestic product (GDP).

As previously noted, parliamentary democracy was terminated for a third time by the coup of June 30, 1989. Once again, political parties, their newspapers, and other free associations were outlawed, and senior politicians were arrested. Within a relatively short period, however, it became clear that the new junta differed greatly from its predecessors in political orientation and style. Far from being a nonpartisan group of military officers simply disgusted with the mismanagement of almost everything, as erroneously reported early on,[6] the RCC-NS had a definite agenda and soon set out to pursue its objectives.

Like all previous Sudanese governments, the Bashir regime faces four major interrelated tasks: political control and government stability without which none of the other items can be addressed; halting the economic tailspin and, at a minimum, improving the daily living standards in such key areas as Khartoum and ports and communications centers; stopping rebellions in the south and other outlying areas and arriving at a comprehensive formula for interregional relations; and managing foreign affairs in such a way that the above objectives can be facilitated.

The interrelatedness of these tasks can be seen in several developments: the national economy has suffered tremendously from governmental instability in Khartoum and from the high cost of the rebellion in the south—some estimates put the cost at $1 million a day; the central government has been paralyzed over issues of sharing power and constitutional reform including the debate over the use of the *sharia*, Western, or customary law codes. The rebellion by the Sudan People's Liberation Army (SPLA)—like its earlier counterpart, the Anya-Nya—appears destined to continue at least as long as these issues remain unresolved. Meanwhile, foreign policy priorities have had to focus on interdicting external support for the rebels while acquiring from abroad military and economic assistance needed to confront them and to wean some tribal groupings in marginal areas away from the SPLA. Precisely because the current regime came to power as an alternative to all its predecessors, it is important in assessing the viability of the RCC-NS to review the records of parliamentary regimes prior to June 1989.

Parliamentary Democracy

In terms of political culture, the Sudanese have ranked among the most democratic in the Arab world and Africa.[7] They have a strong sense of egalitarianism and a tradition of electing tribal and local notables, coupled with an easily observable insistence on verbal give-and-take regardless of rank or position of authority.[8] It is equally easily observable that politically conscious Sudanese disdain authority of any kind and particularly loathe military rule despite—or perhaps because of—having been saddled with three versions for much of their post-independence experience. Multiparty elections in the Sudan have always been open and fair in comparison with other Arab or African states. Such is the belief in free association that elections in 1986 were contested by an astonishing 42 parties and groupings,[9] and there were at least as many nongovernment newspapers and journals. The question asked by many, of course, has been whether such a system is suitable for a country like Sudan, and, if not, what system is.

In Sudan's five multiparty elections for parliament—1953, 1958, 1965, 1968, and 1986—it has been unfortunate that no party ever obtained at least 51 percent of the seats in any election and that, therefore, all governments have been coalitions. The basic reasons for Sudan's political fragmentation, as evidenced by these multiparty elections, are complex, but relatively straightforward. There are five major Islamic sects in the northern Sudan: the Mahdiyyah, Khatmiyya, Hindiyyah, Tijaniyyah, and Qadiriyyah. The first two are the largest by far and, during the nationalist period under the condominium, set up their own political organizations. The Mahdiyyah established the Umma Party, with followers mostly in the central and western regions, and the Khatmiyyah founded the People's Democratic Party (PDP), with followers primarily in the northern and eastern areas. As an antidote to these largely rural-based sects, some civil servants, urban merchants, and university graduates set up the National Unionist Party (NUP) which has drawn electoral support from urban centers. Periodically, the NUP and PDP aligned themselves against what they considered the overwhelming strength of the "House of Mahdi"; from 1968 on, they merged to form the Democratic Unionist Party (DUP), but never lost their separate identities.

In all parliamentary elections the best performance by any party gained 42 percent of the total vote. Together, these three essentially centrist parties never obtained less than three-fourths of the votes and electoral seats. The remainder has consisted of several regional blocs in the south, east, and far west and, since the 1960s, the more radical elements of the political spectrum such as the communists and assorted socialists on the left and the Muslim Brotherhood—as the Islamic Charter Front and now as the National Islamic Front (NIF)—on the right. It is noteworthy that southern parties have never managed to organize effectively throughout the south.[10] This has resulted both in the fragmentation of the southern bloc in parliament into subregional groupings and also in the inability of southern parties to garner all southern constituencies. In fact, a significant number of these empty seats have gone to Umma or NUP affiliates.

What, then, is the problem with parliamentary democracy in the Sudan? A detailed answer can be frustratingly complicated, especially if one gets bogged down in specific actions and reactions by this or that individual or group—another Sudanese characteristic—but a simplified version is possible to construct.

Every coalition government, by definition, has a senior and a junior partner, with portfolios allocated accordingly. Often within months of assuming governing responsibility, the junior partner is approached by the opposition with proposals for a better portfolio arrangement. Sooner or later, the offer becomes too tempting, a vote of confidence is called, and the government falls. The new coalition experiences a certain "honeymoon" period until the former senior partner, now in opposition, begins its own flirtations with one or another grouping to undermine the new partnership. The end effect is twofold: Coalition politics deteriorates into a game of musical chairs and, indeed, during the first six years of democratic rule every possible combination of centrist parties has been in power and each single party has been in opposition.[11] Unfortunately, this pattern has been reinforced by another characteristic of Sudanese politics: Various junior partners have entered coalition governments not only for the understandable interest of sharing power, but also, apparently, often with the unspoken intent of undermining their senior partner while in office. Tactics would include blocking a unified strategy, causing embarrassment to the government by public disagreement on major issues or by any device that prevented the coalition from appearing to be a team and speaking with one voice because credit would then go to the prime minister and to his party.

Precisely because smaller groupings have limited appeal, their calculations have been to discredit all rivals so that in due time the body politic would eventually look to their group as the last best hope. Perhaps even more disastrous for public policy, it appears that an overwhelming proportion of political energy expended in the capital has gone toward undermining or shoring up a coalition and deterrence of such activities, with the result that little attention has been given to, and little energy left for, the major national problems of economics, regional rebellion, and societal transformation.

Given Sudan's history of recurrent military rule, one might think that the lesson of military takeovers following democratic misrule would have been thoroughly learned by all civilian politicians, at the very least by the end of Numayri's 16-year-long dictatorship which they had unanimously denounced. This would seem especially true of Umma Party leader Sadiq al-Mahdi who, as prime minister, had already once been ousted in 1967 by just the sort of maneuvering described above. Furthermore, he had been imprisoned several times and also forced to flee into exile by military governments. Consequently, most observers—foreign and Sudanese—considered this well-educated and highly sophisticated politician to be the most suitable candidate for leading a democratic Sudan in a time of crisis.

Sadiq was quick to organize his party after Numayri's fall and, during the April 1986 elections, gained the most seats: 100 out of 233 territorial constituencies. It is interesting to note, however, that the "graduates" constituencies—reserved for educated voters—were overwhelmingly won, 22 seats out of 28, by the NIF, compared with 2 seats for the Umma Party and 4 for the Communist Party.

As expected, Sadiq became prime minister again and led a series of six successive coalition governments: first with the election's runner-up DUP, then with the third place NIF, once with an all-party (except the Communist Party) "government of national salvation," and others, but all to no avail. The height of futility may have been reached with the coalition stalemate in the latter part of his middle period—August 1987 to May 1988—when the government operated without a cabinet. It consisted only of the state council for official functions, while the daily tasks of ministries were performed under the administration of their respective undersecretaries. Both Sudanese and foreign observers of this spectacle responded with a mixture of bemusement, ridicule (in private and in the media), and increasing anger. As for the government, even though issues such as economic development and reform, and especially resolution of the civil war, were publicly discussed at great length, little concrete action ensued.

Economics and Politics

Since the early 1960s, Sudan's national revenue has declined, a result not only of the scarcity of capital and export earnings, but also because of such political decisions as bloating the civil service with university graduates in the lower ranks while frightening into exile many competent senior officials through repeated purges going back as far as October 1964. Similarly, ideas spawned by the October Revolution triggered a significant conversion of local government policy. Junior bureaucrats were now being assigned to administer outlying areas in the name of "progressive modernization," thus replacing the more experienced and respected tribal chieftains of the so-called Native Administration system under British tutelage. The change caused a sharp decline in local tax revenue collection in the rural areas—90 percent of the country.

By the early 1970s the concept of turning Sudan into the food basket of the Arab world had gained sufficient currency to lure huge Western and Arab investments, both public and private. Mismanagement by Numayri's bureaucracy and the growing practice of corruption in high places were viewed as delaying and undercutting many development schemes. With productivity in all sectors declining, debts began to mount, and, by the time of Numayri's overthrow, the size of Sudan's foreign debt—then about $10 billion, by mid-1990 more than $12 billion—had actually exceeded the country's entire GDP for one year. This meant that all available foreign exchange had to be diverted for debt servicing of interest obligations. The governments have repeatedly been warned by their creditors that they were facing bankruptcy. All governments from the Transitional Military Council (TMC) under Siwar al-Dhahab to the RCC-NS recognized the gravity of the economic situation, but the TMC felt helpless to initiate major reforms, and civilian politicians merely declared the debts to be "Numayri's debts."

Foreign donors were also facing financial problems, and this factor compounded Sudan's economic situation. The Arab Gulf states experienced dramatic declines in oil revenues in the mid-1980s while simultaneously under pressure from obligations such as offering financial support to Iraq in its war with Iran. The US government, caught in the throes of the Gramm-Rudman budget deficit legislation, was unable to meet even the assistance levels of previous years, and since the Bashir takeover, US military and development assistance has been cut altogether.[12] Nevertheless, considerable humanitarian relief assistance and food aid have continued.

Throughout the 1980s hopes had been high that the Chevron oil fields, with sizable proven reserves in the southwest, would eventually produce enough revenue for import substitution and some additional export. This potential source for reversing economic deterioration has not materialized as yet because Chevron's management was forced to halt construction on the pipeline from Bentiu to the projected refinery in Kosti (and beyond to the shipping terminal of Port Sudan) as a result of attacks on its work crews by the members of the SPLA, especially in 1984. Here the link between economic recovery and domestic security becomes clear. The SPLA had targeted the pipeline construction before the 1985 coup mainly to prevent the possibility that Chevron oil revenues would "rescue the tottering Numayri dictatorship," according to repeated pronouncements by John Garang, leader of the Sudan People's Liberation Movement (SPLM) and its military arm, the SPLA, on the clandestine SPLA Radio.

The Politics of Religion

With the departure of Numayri, SPLA fighting was expected to cease, but that did not happen. Despite many well-meaning overtures to Garang by the transitional prime minister, Jazuli Dafa'allah, in 1985—and one year later similar offers from his successor, Sadiq al-Mahdi—to meet at any available conference site, and negotiate any issue, complete with verbal and written assurances that the government had no intention of subjugating or discriminating against southerners in any way, Garang refused to accept such promises as genuine. In broadcast after broadcast, the SPLA labeled the TMC an extension of Numayri's military dictatorship but without Numayri.[13]

Many observers agree that the first few months after the April uprising presented several opportunities for resolving the conflict between the central government and the SPLM/SPLA. For that period through Sadiq's first six months in office, it is difficult not to place the greater blame on Garang's uncompromising hard line, though it perhaps resulted from faulty intelligence transmitted by his informants in the capital area. Given traditional distrust between northerners and southerners, one can easily imagine a suspicious mind misreading a potentially workable proposal. On the other hand, Garang could point to Khartoum's refusal to lift the highly sensitive "September Laws" as a good-faith gesture.[14] The TMC felt this was the province of a constituent assembly and would therefore be inappropriate for it to do. Whether the TMC actually believed in this position or not is difficult to judge, but one strongly suspects that the devout Prime Minister Dafa'allah and TMC chairman General Siwar al-Dhahab felt uncomfortable entering Sudanese history—and, more widely, that of the Islamic world—as the individuals who revoked the sharia.

Well before the 1986 elections were held, Sadiq al-Mahdi had been the first prominent politician publicly to declare his opposition to the 1983 laws. Although many members of the DUP had voiced similar reservations closer to the elections, the party had taken no official position on the matter. Once it joined the first coalition government, however, the DUP hesitated to consider abrogation. The DUP's stance may have reflected any or all of the following: disorganization among the party's factions; concern about future voter reaction, particularly in view of strident NIF charges of "un-Islamic conduct"; and possibly the opportunity to embarrass the prime minister indirectly through lack of cooperation in the hope of future gains at Umma Party expense. Ironically, two and one-half years later, the DUP called for suspension of the sharia during an Umma-NIF coalition.

Predictably, the NIF championed the sharia while southerners saw these laws as evidence of northern cultural imperialism. Increasingly,

Sadiq became less outspoken about abrogation of Numayri's September Laws and called for "alternative laws" based on "true Islamic values" to replace them. Many observers, including southern politicians and foreign governments, became impatient with the spectacle of apparently conflicting statements repeated in various formats for what seemed an inordinate number of months. The issue came to a preliminary head in September 1988 when the coalition government submitted to parliament a draft bill for new Islamic legislation that produced a domestic stalemate and foreign uproar. Partially to resolve the stalemate, the DUP leadership met with the SPLM in Ethiopia, and the two sides produced an agreement in November, only to be snubbed by Sadiq. Because the content of the agreement seemed identical to Sadiq's own earlier stated position, one might conclude that his opposition to the DUP-SPLM agreement was based more on jealousy than substance. As much as anything else, Sadiq's action—or lack thereof—hastened the crucial events that would occur in February and March 1989.

To the SPLM, however, these developments were proof that Sadiq's government was not serious about addressing southern grievances. This belief was reinforced when the central government decided to arm tribal militias in areas bordering on SPLA strongholds, especially in the south of Kordofan and Darfur where there had been historic rivalries with Dinkas who, though part of a southern tribe, live in these areas. Both sides rationalized their positions. Khartoum reminded all parties that the central government had an obligation to maintain law and order and to protect citizens endangered by the rebel "outlaws"; the rebels justified their attacks on garrisoned towns because of the Khartoum government's alleged bad faith as demonstrated by these actions. Such statements, frequently heard on radio interviews, in effect became policy. While the fighting continued sporadically, some dialogue continued just as sporadically behind the scenes through intermediaries traveling to East African cities. A cynical observer might consider this situation an acceptable level of low-intensity violence because of the longstanding tradition of sporadic tribal warfare between the Dinka in southwest Sudan and the adjacent Rizeigat and Messirriyah tribes. In this context, even the occurrence of three unusually large massacres of Dinka in March, August, and September 1987 was not entirely surprising, although they were dutifully deplored by both parties.[15]

The term "acceptable level of violence" could not be used to characterize another event that left deep psychological scars among many. On the morning of August 16, 1986, a Sudanese civilian airliner was shot down just after take-off from Malakal[16] airport by a SAM-7 missile fired by the SPLA; all 57 passengers and a crew of 3 perished. During the next several days the SPLM/SPLA not only acknowledged the act, but also blamed the Khartoum government for ignoring the SPLA warning that it would shoot down any aircraft, military or civilian, even if on a famine relief mission. It justified this policy by claiming that relief planes (and subsequently train and truck convoys) were used to smuggle weapons to the army and to supply government soldiers rather than famine victims with food. Interestingly, the SPLA statement insisted that this measure "should not be perceived as being directed against the Koka Dam negotiating process."[17]

A quite different response came from Khartoum where the prime minister branded Garang and his movement "terrorist,"[18] and his chief spokesman in parliament declared that the act was the "language of war" and that "this is the language the government will use from now on in dealing with Garang and his movement, the SPLA."[19] As far as the government was concerned, Garang had earlier turned down all reasonable proposals for meetings and discussions of mutual problems. Even so, as an act of good faith, Khartoum decided to keep the door open for dialogue despite the rejections. After the downing of the airliner, however, and the self-righteous defense of it, the government felt justified in closing the door and putting the onus for reopening it on the SPLM.

From the SPLM/SPLA perspective, however, the central issue has been adherence to the Koka Dam agreement of March 1986. The agreement resulted from meetings at Koka Dam, Ethiopia, with representatives of the SPLM/SPLA, the National Alliance for Professionals, and major political parties with the exception of the DUP. It called for the "creation of a new Sudan . . . free from racism, tribalism, sectarianism and all causes of discrimination and disparity . . . " and "for lifting the state of emergency, for repealing the September 1983 (Islamic) laws, for adopting the 1956 constitution as amended in 1964, and for the abrogation of military pacts signed by the previous regime."[20] With regard to the military conflict in the south, both parties stated that they "would genuinely endeavor to stop the bloodshed resulting from war in the Sudan . . . " and "call for a ceasefire" and, subsequently, for a constitutional conference to be held in Khartoum during the third week of June 1986 with an agreed-upon, nine-point agenda.[21]

Almost immediately after the announcement of the Koka Dam declaration, Garang clarified his interpretation of it at a high-level meeting of his top lieutenants, as reported by the clandestine SPLA Radio. One significant aspect concerned SPLM/SPLA policy toward the then imminent elections, which he termed as "partial, therefore resulting in a partial government in Khartoum, representing one side of the country and . . . not in line with the people's hopes for building a new Sudan where nobody will be taken for granted."[22]

The impression has lingered that Garang and the SPLM leadership have considered the Koka Dam declaration a pronouncement of their philosophical views and a policy statement of their conditions for peace negotiations with Khartoum. By contrast, northern politicians seem to have seen Koka Dam as a concession to Garang necessary to persuade him to agree to a cease-fire but not necessarily as a policy platform for the final resolution of the conflict.

What is clear is that the rebel leadership understood racism to mean Arab versus African discrimination. The rejection of "tribalism, sectarianism," and so forth, referred to political parties based on sectarian identity such as the Umma Party and the DUP and regionalism such as the Nuba Mountain, Beja, and Fur political party groupings. Other clauses, such as those claiming that basic problems were national rather than north-south issues and Garang's repeated calls for a "revolutionary socialist" Sudan point to the SPLM's intent to define not only the reason for conflict in terms other than north versus south, but also the solution.

At a minimum, this solution denied the legitimacy of the April 1986 elections and, in general, the legitimacy of the existing party structure.

To admit such a position would be unacceptable to northern parties inasmuch as it would lead to their dissolution. Yet, given Sudan's demographics and the resulting preponderance of northern-based parties in the country, southerners have no realistic chance of coming to power within the prevailing system. At the same time, given the central government's inability to defeat the rebellion by military force alone, the stalemate between northern politicians and southern rebels could theoretically go on forever.

New Politics

In February and March 1989 all these crises came to a head. Defense Minister Abd al-Majid Hamad al-Khalil resigned, and the armed forces commander in chief, General Fathi Ahmad Ali, presented Prime Minister Sadiq al-Mahdi with a petition signed by 150 officers demanding major reforms in domestic, foreign, and security policies. This de facto ultimatum brought about a number of changes, but at the expense of dropping the NIF from an all-party government because of the latter's refusal to agree to the suspension of the sharia until the convening of a constitutional conference.

Three months later, when it appeared that the long-delayed conference with the SPLM/SPLA would finally take place, and all necessary concessions had apparently been made and were scheduled for cabinet approval on 1 July, military officers led by Umar al-Bashir executed their coup within hours. This chronological sequence has led many observers to conclude that the coup was an NIF operation designed to thwart the abrogation of the long-cherished sharia. Such an interpretation has been vehemently denied by the new rulers who pointed to political, economic, and security chaos in the south and in western Sudan where local militias, Chadians, and Libyan agents had been running amok. Perhaps to support this argument, the junta arrested NIF leader Hassan al-Turabi along with other civilian politicians and placed him in solitary confinement. This observer tends to agree with those who consider this maneuver a clever subterfuge allowing Turabi undetected coordination of RCC-NS policy decisions from his cell, while some believe that a younger NIF wing, critical of Turabi's pragmatism, influenced key RCC-NS members to restrict his actions for a time. In any case, whereas most Sudanese have debated these rival interpretations almost to distraction, the more important result is the obviously pro-NIF orientation and policy of the RCC-NS.

During their first year in power, the new rulers changed the atmosphere of politics in Sudan drastically. There can be no doubt about the seriousness of purpose with which they pursue their agenda. Individual meetings with senior members of the RCC-NS, including President Bashir, revealed a tough and determined attitude, as have the no-nonsense approaches to initial policy formulations in rather marked contrast to the waverings of Numayri's decision-making style. Equally clear is an obvious distrust of civilian politicians—not only those associated with the now discredited former parties, but also their own civilian cabinet officers whose freedom of action seems limited to executing decisions from above and to formal management of their bureaucracies.

Within the ministries, RCC-NS interference is highly visible, most directly in the large-scale purges of civil servants deemed to have unacceptable political affiliations or tendencies. Whereas previous regimes, such as the October 1964 group and Numayri's in his several stages, have also purged senior officials with obvious or strongly perceived ties to opposing groups, never before have the numbers of those purged from the civil and foreign services, the professions, and universities been so large, nor the grounds for dismissal as clearly ideological. The enemy list apparently contains, above all, anyone with known or presumed, present or past, communist affiliation and those accused of corruption, immorality, alcoholism, and illegal dealings in foreign currencies. Those knowledgeable about the Muslim Brotherhood and other Islamist organizations throughout the world immediately recognize these code-words.

In a slightly different, but related context, President Bashir has committed himself to root out all those government employes responsible for low productivity or passive resistance to public policy.[23] Indeed, new attendance rules have been issued and are enforced strictly, even by surprise visits of RCC-NS members. The often summary nature of the dismissals has led many critics to complain about arbitrariness and ideological purging, but the regime defends its actions as necessary for instilling a long-abandoned work ethic. Another example of departure from old-style politics is the RCC-NS's declared attitude toward political participation. In statements and interviews, the leader of the political committee and the president have repeatedly restated their commitment to popular participation and described rule by their junta as only a transitional and necessary step for establishing order. Bashir spoke of a three-stage process for popular participation to create political awareness and discussion at the local level. After the groundwork has been completed, the ruling junta would in theory withdraw, somewhat "akin to the Turkish model."[24] As recently as May 26, 1990, RCC-NS member Colonel Salah al-Din Karrar said in a press statement that a civilian government would be formed in early 1991 to prepare the country for political pluralism and free elections.[25] He also made clear, however, as Bashir has done on many occasions, that there will be no return to the previous party organizations, but that "people may opt for the three or four political forums representing different political colors and there should be a charter to govern the press."[26]

When challenged about the apparent inconsistency of a commitment to popular political participation in the face of military repression and purges, junta members have unhesitatingly responded that they do not believe in Western-style liberal democracy—which they see as divisive and dysfunctional in a country like Sudan—but in a "more appropriate" form of democracy via citizens' committees, by which they apparently mean *shura* (consultation). As an interim measure, the RCC-NS has appointed several committees of 30 to 40 advisers each in specialized areas such as economics, social issues, and regional administration. Committee leaders are mainly technocrats from the Numayri era.

The RCC-NS also frequently points to a tolerance for varied and opposing points of view, as long as these are confined to debate and are not antigovernment conspiracies. Their main exhibit is the National Dialogue Conference of September and October 1989, to which all political groupings were invited. Nearly all groups sent representatives to the conference in Khartoum's Friendship Hall except the SPLM/

SPLA. The most important sessions took place in the Committee on Options for the Future in which positions from left to center to right could be heard and rather sophisticated discussions of the jurisdictions and interrelationships in a federal system could be observed. In the end, the National Dialogue Conference produced a plan for a confederated Sudan, and the RCC-NS presented the 50-plus page document to the rebel leadership as well as to selected foreign governments (including the United States) for diplomatic support.

As of summer 1990, the RCC-NS has been no more successful in bringing Garang to the negotiating table than were its three predecessor governments, despite its publicly stated commitment to end the war. There remains a deeply held conviction by many in and out of government that Garang's alleged communist leanings explain his intransigence. Garang holds similar negative views of his adversaries, seeing them as a group of "junior officers" wielding illegitimate power.

The drama of casualties on both sides and attendant suffering by innocent civilians has been interrupted occasionally by prospects for compromise, often after international intervention to support relief efforts. This occasional cooperation constitutes the high point. The low point, too often, has been the refusal of both sides to permit relief activities on the excuse that food and other supplies go to government and rebel soldiers instead of to famine victims.

The specter of stalemate in the war, coupled with ever harsher economic conditions throughout the country—including long lines for bread and gasoline—and the inability of the regime to gain consistent foreign support, except from Libya, have combined to produce an atmosphere of despair. Add to this the talk in Khartoum about new purges and jails overflowing with political prisoners, whether correct or not, and rumors of torture and other human rights abuses (according to Amnesty International and Africa Watch), all against the backdrop of a nightly curfew and the growing presence of internal security forces. It is fair to conclude that Sudanese society has been polarized as never before. Those who support the regime do so enthusiastically, praising the return of discipline to government offices and to social behavior at large and welcoming the sharia as a blueprint for society—the alternative to everything tried before. Almost everyone else is in opposition, including those northern Muslims who prefer traditional religious and social organizations. The traditional center seems to have disappeared.

It is not surprising that opposition to the RCC-NS is considerable and ranges from the personal to the systemic to the ideological. Whereas the SPLA continues to fight Khartoum from the south, northern opposition to the government evolved from passive resistance through inaction in government offices to contacts among exiles abroad, until in early 1990 a formal alliance, the National Democratic Grouping, was forged by leaders from both north, especially the Umma Party, and south.

Within the military, opposition coalesced into two coup plots and one alleged attempt in March and April 1990. The most significant challenge occurred at dawn on April 23, 1990, when a group of military officers, including three brigadier generals, allegedly tried to take over key government installations. The efforts were foiled, and the plotters were arrested, tried, and executed within 24 hours. Regime critics abroad almost immediately protested that the alleged coup may have been stage-managed by the RCC-NS to eliminate opposition, and they pointed to the arrest several days earlier of three of the executed officers. They also lodged charges of unfair trials—some cases allegedly lasting only a few minutes—without right to independent counsel or witnesses. The RCC-NS replied that all military officers, including those retired, were subject to military law, that they were caught in the act of plotting, and were judged accordingly. In subsequent interviews, the impression was left that at least some ringleaders were Baathists who had long conspired to seize power. Be that as it may, public opinion in Sudan was shocked by the rapidity and severity of the junta's response—precisely the desired effect. To quote President Bashir, "In order that these coup attempts do not recur, and to maintain the country's stability and reputation, deterrent and tough sentences were required. . . . "[27]

No doubt this message has been received, but there can also be no doubt that it has further hardened the already polarized positions in contemporary Sudanese politics.[28] It is highly unlikely that there will soon be a return to the old days of conversational give-and-take and the occasional nonviolent street demonstration chasing a military regime out of office. Sudanese politics, which regardless of governmental system had long been characterized by egalitarianism and a relatively gentlemanly set of rules, may have finally been transformed. The previous tradition of reluctant acceptance of those with different beliefs, ethnic background, and life-styles has been replaced by intolerance for all dissenters.

Long-time observers of Sudan could always be confident that the country's distinct political culture would spare it the authoritarianisms of an Ethiopia or an Iraq, other ethnically heterogeneous countries with regional insurrections. As this article has tried to show, the evolution of political developments in the 1980s has created a new style of politics in Sudan, whether for better or for worse, and these long-time observers may not recognize the country anymore.

NOTES

1. The Arab Fund for Economic and Social Development (AFESD) in the mid-1970s earmarked several billion dollars for projects to turn Sudan into the "food basket of the Arab World." The Kuwaiti Fund (KFAED) similarly funded numerous projects in Sudan. Much earlier the United Nations had identified Sudan as one of only three Third World countries with good developmental potential. United Nations, *Population Growth and Manpower in the Sudan*, Series A/37 (New York: United Nations, 1964).

2. These uprisings occurred October 21, 1964, and again on April 5, 1985, when the Ibrahim Abbud and Numayri dictatorships were overthrown. For details see, *inter alia.*, Peter Bechtold, *Politics in the Sudan* (New York: Praeger, 1976), pp. 211–19, and idem, "Sudan since the Fall of Numayri," in Robert O. Freedman, ed., *The Middle East from the Iran-Contra Affair to the Intifada* (Syracuse, NY: Syracuse University Press, forthcoming December 1990).

3. The Constituent Assembly was elected prior to independence in late 1953 to discuss the future status of the country.

4. A portion of a statement broadcast on Radio Omdurman, November 17, 1958.

5. This rebellion escalated into civil war, pitting much of the south against

the northern-dominated government in Khartoum until it was resolved by the March 1972 Addis Ababa agreement which granted regional autonomy to the south.

6. Early reports from key Arab and Western embassies described the junta as nonpartisan and composed of political independents.

7. This perhaps startling conclusion results from this author's almost 30 years of study of Sudan and from professional visits and field research in 20 countries of the Middle East and North Africa.

8. For example, a cabinet officer will not look down on or talk down to a driver or a cook, and this attitude extends similarly throughout society.

9. Only about 12 of these represent major political, regional, or ideological factions; the rest are splinter groups. Another issue is the degree to which these parties resemble those in other parliamentary systems inasmuch as only a few of them aim at a national constituency and have a truly national agenda.

10. These include the Liberal Party, Black Bloc, Sudan African National Union (SANU), and Southern Front.

11. For example, the combination of NUP-PDP, Umma-PDP, and Umma-NUP. In addition, all governments to this day have included a few southern cabinet members, usually one each from Upper Nile, Bahr al-Ghazal, and Equatoria regions. They, in turn, were seen by some southerners as quislings.

12. The aid cutoff was in accordance with a congressional mandate (Section 513 of the US Foreign Assistance Act of 1986) to halt assistance to all countries where democratically elected governments have been overthrown.

13. SPLA Radio as reported by Foreign Broadcast Information Service (FBIS)—Middle East and Africa (MEA), May 1985, *passim.*

14. These laws, based on the sharia, had been introduced by the Numayri regime in September 1983 and were applied on a national scale—as opposed to just Muslim areas—to the consternation of many, both at home and abroad, Muslim and non-Muslim.

15. In March 1987, several hundred Dinka men, women, an children— some say as many as a thousand—were killed at Al-Diein in southern Darfur by a mob of Rizeigat tribesmen. On August 11–12, 1987, and again during September 6–11, 1987, between 1,000 and 2,000 Dinka civilians were re- portedly killed by army and militia forces in Wau, Bahr al-Ghazal Province. This followed an attempted missile attack on a government aircraft and was accompanied by the killings of Fertit militiamen by Dinkas. Amnesty Inter- national, *Sudan: Human Rights Developments since 1985* (New York: Am- nesty International, 1988), p. 5.

16. Capital of Upper Nile, the northern-most province of southern Sudan.

17. From FBIS-MEA, August 18, 1986, p. i. The Koka Dam meetings in Ethiopia were held to resolve differences and end the civil war. The agreement was signed on March 24, 1986.

18. From Sudan News Agency, as reported in FBIS-MEA, August 21, 1986, p. Q2.

19. *Ibid.*, p. Q5.

20. FBIS-MEA, April 1, 1986, pp. Q7–8.

21. *Ibid.*

22. SPLA Radio, March 29, 1986, as reported in FBIS-MEA, April 1, 1986, p. Q7.

23. Interview with President Bashir at the presidential palace, September 27, 1989.

24. *Ibid.*

25. Kuwait News Agency, May 26, 1990, as reported by FBIS-Near East and South Asia, June 4, 1990, p. 20.

26. *Ibid.*

27. Excerpt from lengthy interview by Kamal Bakhit, *al-Watan al-Arabi*, May 18, 1990, pp. 16–19.

28. According to reliable sources, anger about the summary executions was even exceeded by rumors about some of the alleged details, such as refusal to say prayers and to hand the bodies over to relatives. Factually correct or not, the rumor mill will have done its damage in this highly sensitive society.

War of Visions for the Nation

Francis Mading Deng

The war that has been raging intermittently in Sudan for more than three decades has generally been perceived as a cleavage between the dominant and more developed Arabized Muslim north—two-thirds of the land and population of the country—and the subordinated, less developed, but potentially richer African south, predominantly traditional in its religious beliefs with a Christianized modern leadership. While this provides a useful starting point, it oversimplifies a more complex situation, for Sudan is a country in which myths have been highlighted to overshadow the realities of the national identity in its racial, cultural, and religious diversity. Recently, the war has been crystallizing into an ideological confrontation between Islamists and secularists, a development that has injected yet another element of oversimplification, but is also redrawing the map of political alignments across the south-north dividing line. As a result of this conflict, Sudan has largely failed to live up to its postulated role as an Afro-Arab microcosm and a strategic link between the continent and the Middle East.

The conflict erupted in August 1955 when a mutiny by one southern battalion was triggered by a widely shared fear in the south that independence was going to mean a change of masters—from the British to the Arabs—and could entail the return of the slave trade in which blacks were the victims of the Arab north. The mutineers were eventually persuaded to lay down their arms when the outgoing British governor general promised justice. When the northern parties also pledged to give serious consideration to the southern call for a federal system of government, the country united behind the declaration of independence on January 1, 1956.

It soon became evident, however, that the north was not intent on honoring the pledge for a federal constitution, but, quite the contrary, sought to impose Arabization and Islamization on the south in an attempt to achieve national unity through uniformity. There was even a serious call in the north for the adoption of an Islamic constitution.[1] In response, hostilities were reactivated under the leadership of the Southern Sudan Liberation Movement (SSLM), better known as Anya-Nya, its military arm. Its objective was the secession of the south and the establishment of an independent state.[2] In 1972, however, the movement agreed with the military government of Jaafar al-Numayri on a compromise solution, the Addis Ababa agreement that granted the south regional autonomy.[3]

It was Numayri's unilateral abrogation of the Addis Ababa agreement—by dividing the south into three regions with reduced constitutional powers, and then, in alliance with the Muslim Brotherhood, imposing the so-called September [Islamic] Laws—that led to the resumption of hostilities in 1983 by the leadership of the Sudan People's Liberation Movement (SPLM) and its military wing, the Sudan People's Liberation Army (SPLA). The declared objective of the SPLM/SPLA is not the secession or even the autonomy of the south, but the creation of a new Sudan, united and free of racial, religious, cultural, or gender discrimination.[4]

Two years after hostilities resumed, Numayri was overthrown by a popular uprising in 1985. A transitional government coaxed the country back to parliamentary democracy within a year, but military rule returned on June 30, 1989, in a coup led by previously unknown middle-ranking officers proclaiming a "Revolution of National Salvation." The changes in government have not led to the abrogation of the infamous September Laws, one of the conditions of the SPLM/SPLA, the argument being that in Islam there is no separation between religion and state and therefore no Muslim ruler would dare to abrogate Islamic law.

As a result of these developments, the conflict has increasingly been viewed in religious terms. Although this has the effect of oversimplifying the situation, it makes religion symbolic of all that is contested, a critical factor in the definition of the national identity and in the shaping and sharing of power, wealth, development opportunities, and foreign policy. As a consequence, the unity of the country is becoming increasingly accepted, while religion, paradoxically, is becoming a highly divisive factor.[5]

These contradictions make the realities of the Sudanese situation stand in sharp contrast to the lofty ideals proclaimed for the country. Far from being a moderating factor and a strategic link between Africa and the Middle East, Sudan has increasingly become an embarrassment in African-Arab relations; yet, developments have taken place in both the north and the south that make for a fluidity that ironically still promises potential progress toward a united pluralistic Sudan.

Emerging Diversity in the North

In this context, the main development is the lively debate that is taking place regarding national identity and its implications for peace and unity. It is now becoming increasingly recognized that the tendency to identify the north as Arab and Islamic and to contrast it with the "animist," "Christian" south presupposes a degree of racial, cultural, and religious homogeneity that oversimplifies and falsifies a dynamic picture of pluralism with internal differences and potential for realignment across the dividing line. Historical and contemporary realities tell us that while Arabic is spoken throughout the north and Islam is the religion of the overwhelming majority, northerners still see themselves largely in terms of "tribes," many of whom have retained their indigenous languages, some of whom look racially quite negroid, and most of whom practice a version of Islam that is far from orthodox. Few northerners can indeed claim to be homogeneously Arab.[6]

During the post-colonial debate about the various dimensions of the southern problem, elites, especially from the north, used to argue against the characterization of the problem as racial, economic, or even religious. They would point to anomalies of color and other physical characteristics on both sides of the dividing line to support their contention that the problem of the south was not racial. They would also allude to economic conditions in certain areas within the north to refute the claim of north-south disparity as a root cause of the problem. Religious affiliations across the dividing line were also cited to counter allegations of Islamic-Christian confrontation or conflict.

Although reflecting the truth of the situation to a significant degree, these arguments were mostly attempts to confuse and overshadow the factors on the other side of the reality: that, as an attitude of mind rather than an issue of color or physical characteristics, most northerners saw themselves as culturally and even racially Arab; that the north was relatively better off economically than the south; and that, in religious terms, not only were northerners predominantly Muslim and southerners were either believers in indigenous religions or a converted Christian elite, but that it was the deliberate policy of the north to Islamize and Arabize the south. Today, however, the reality appears to be rising to a level of consciousness among Sudanese on both sides. That reality is now more believable because it is being sincerely acknowledged rather than merely manipulated.

Once the uniting myths of northern homogeneity in regard to Islam and Arab race and culture were exposed, new forces surfaced that are now offering opportunities for a more dynamic process of realignments. This trend is more visible in those regions where non-Arab characteristics that cut across the north-south dividing line are apparent. Equally significant, however, is the impact of these regional dynamics on the attitude of the traditional political parties at the national level that are now beginning to see their long-term interests, if not survival, in the degree to which they cater to the legitimate concerns of the regions.[7]

A potential force for national consensus-building across party or regional divisions is the constituency of intellectuals, professional associations, and trade unions that are outside partisan politics, uncommitted to either of the dominant traditional parties. This constituency is becoming increasingly aware not only of the stakes confronting the country, but also of its potential and, indeed, responsibility to play a constructive role in shaping the destiny of the nation. This constituency has also remained largely committed to the substantive principles of liberal democracy rather than to the procedural formula of elections and the rule of automatic majority, guided by blind devotion to sectarian religious leaders.

The Vision from the South

To understand more fully the identities in conflict, it is important to have a better appreciation of the manner in which traditional religions in the south have interplayed with Christianity to produce the attitude that currently resists the spread of Islam southward. Religious attitudes should be viewed in the context of the cultural values prevailing in the country. Despite ethnic, cultural, and religious differences between the north and the south, the fundamental values that shape the attitude of the people in both parts of the country are, surprisingly, not as different as people often assume. In both cases, traditional belief in the values of ancestral continuity tends to constrain innovation, favor conservatism, and engender ethnocentrism and chauvinism.[8] Even with respect to the relationship between religion and the state, the attitudes of Islam and traditional African religions are not dissimilar.

There are, however, two main differences between the two subcultures. Among the southern peoples, the relations between human beings and God are intermediated by their ancestors and clan spirits in an autonomous, personalized, though hierarchical, relationship. In Islam, the system is centralized with God's representatives on earth—Muhammad, or his successors, the imams—as the unchallengable rulers. While in southern belief systems, God is perceived in familial terms as the ultimate father and all human beings are God's children, in Islam, God is the master and human beings are God's slaves. Because no family can impose belief in its ancestral or clan spirits on others, there was a form of religious freedom among the traditional peoples of the south. In Islam, while the *ahl al-dhimma*, the People of the Book, had a recognized, albeit lower, status in the Islamic state, non-believers had none, and those Muslims who dared to disavow the faith could be executed for apostasy.[9]

There is another sense in which the south differs from the north and that is the extent to which the colonial government respected and preserved Islamic Arab values and practices in the north while it introduced, through missionary education, the southern elite to the values and principles of the Christian West, particularly with respect to separation between religion and the state.

Initially, southerners, particularly the traditional elders, did not see conversion to Christianity as a religious or spiritual transformation; it was seen, instead, as a means of acquiring from the missionaries modern education, medicine, and, eventually, employment opportunities. Christianity was considered a means of enhancing physical and spiritual well-being in a manner similar to the purpose of traditional religion, which aims not at securing an everlasting life still to come, but rather at ensuring the prolongation and the quality of life in this world. Elders took the religious conversion of their children from their traditional faith as a price to pay for modern advantages, especially as they did not really believe their children were seriously disavowing their ancestral beliefs. Their traditional representatives continued to pray to their ancestors and to God to protect their partially alienated children.

Ultimately, two religious identities and value-systems, traditional and Christian, converged in the educated southern convert. This composite identity of the educated southerner was represented not only as different from, but also as adverse to, the Arab-Islamic identity and value system of the north. Northerners were also perceived as antagonistic to the introduction of Christianity in the south. Religious intolerance and apprehension about possible persecution by the Muslim north were projected as threats looming over the post-independence south. The subsequent policies of Arabization and Islamization adopted by successive governments after independence confirmed these fears and had the paradoxical effect of reinforcing identification with Christianity as a means of confronting and resisting Muslim-Arab assimilation.

These policies were intended to reverse what the colonial masters had done by filling the supposed religious vacuum of the traditional society with Islam instead of Christianity.[10] If missionaries from far-off Europe could implant their alien religion in the southern context, why should it not be possible for the closer, culturally more familiar

Arab Muslims of the north to do likewise? No attempt was made to understand what the religious or spiritual values of the southerners were and how they had interacted with Christianity and accommodated each other, nor did northerners scrutinize their own image among southerners in light of the historical experiences between the two parts of the country.

Indeed, the acceptance of Christianity and the resistance to Islam in the south could be associated with the contrasting images of British and northern intervention in that part of the country. Once the initial resistance to British occupation was overcome, what the new rulers became known for was their establishment of law and order, their administration of justice, and their system of indirect rule that respected and protected the autonomy of the local communities. In due course, the British came to be viewed as benefactors rather than as oppressors. Although they did little to develop the south economically, aspirations for such development were then still foreign to communities and therefore did not figure in their initial appraisal of British rule.

The image of the northerners, whether prior to colonial rule or since independence, has not enjoyed a similar appreciation; indeed, the reverse has been the case. With independence, the upheavals of the nineteenth century have increasingly returned—violence, oppression, and aggravated animosity have been the pattern rather than the exception. Even the southern fear that slavery would return after independence became tragically justified as the use of Arab militias by the government to help fight the SPLM/SPLA unleashed an unscrupulous hunt for captives among the rural population of the south.[11] Whatever religious or cultural values are associated with such an order are likely to be stigmatized and resisted. This resistance should not, however, be mistaken for a conservative commitment to the existing tribally-oriented structures that were affirmed and utilized by the British administration. Quite the contrary, the south has witnessed a complex transformation that combined ethnic and cultural self-assertiveness with a widening sense of political vision.

By far the most significant development is the degree to which the southern leadership has extended its vision beyond the south's horizon

to the national level. Although the SPLM and the SPLA are still seen
as southern, their postulated goal is one of creating a new Sudan free
from all forms of discrimination, an objective that is shared not only
by other regional groups, but also by liberal, progressive Sudanese.

Competing Visions for the Nation

Paradoxically, while the vision from the south has been expanding
along unitary lines, the role of religion has emerged as the central
source of disagreement in the conflict, and northern protagonists for
an Islamic state have come into direct confrontation with the secularists, led by the SPLM/SPLA, over competing visions for the nation.

Following Numayri's overthrow, the Muslim Brotherhood reorga-
nized itself into a broader-based political party, the National Islamic
Front (NIF), which won a third position in parliamentary elections.
Their Islamic national agenda was endorsed and significantly reinforced by the June 1989 military coup. After a period of silence, os-
tensibly to study the situation, the SPLM/SPLA condemned the coup
as an Islamist move engineered by the NIF and secretly committed to
the division of the country along religious lines. They did agree, however, to hold peace talks with the government.[12] As of June 1990, the
parties had held two unsuccessful meetings, the first in Addis Ababa,
August 19–20, 1989, and the second in Nairobi, December 1–5, 1989.
Between September 9 and October 21, 1989, the government convened
a National Dialogue Conference on peace issues which completed its
work with the principal recommendation of a federal constitution as
the appropriate framework for solving the country's problems of regional, ethnic, cultural, and religious diversity. The recommendations
of the conference were endorsed by the government and recognized by
the SPLM/SPLA, along with recommendations from other sources, as
providing useful bases for constitutional talks.[13] With respect to third-
party mediation, much has been going on that has involved many actors
on both regional and international levels, but no appreciable progress
has been made on the peace front beyond agreement on such gener-

alities as preservation of the unity of the country, adoption of a federal system of government, and correction of past inequities in economic and social development among the regions.

Meanwhile, the identification of the regime with the NIF has continued to be substantiated, and, in retrospect, is explained in terms of the circumstances leading to the military intervention on June 30, 1989. The reason often given to justify the allegation that the coup was plotted by the NIF is that it aborted what appeared to have been a peace momentum that would have removed the religious obstacle to productive negotiations. It had become obvious to the leaders of the dominant political parties that they could no longer ignore the national outcry for peace and the popular demand for serious talks with the SPLM/SPLA. Whether in response to this demand, or in a tactical move to undercut the dominant Umma Party and the NIF, then the coalition partners in the government, the Democratic Unionist Party (DUP)—the second largest party which was then in the opposition—entered into a dialogue with the SPLM/SPLA and reached a peace accord that was signed by their respective leaders, Muhammad Uthman al-Mirghani and John Garang, on November 16, 1988. The terms of the agreement were similar to those of the Koka Dam declaration of March 1986 initially agreed to by all parties except the DUP and NIF. They involved "freezing" the September Laws, abrogation of defense pacts with foreign countries, lifting the state of emergency, a cease-fire, and preparation for a national constitutional conference.[14] The agreement was well received by the people of Sudan.

With the DUP reaching a separate agreement comparable to the Koka Dam declaration, only the NIF remained outside the peace process and was indeed hostile to the progress made because of its compromise on the issue of the *sharia*. The Umma Party, which was committed to some form or Islamic law, also opposed the accord. With their parliamentary majority, the Umma Party and NIF moved the Constituent Assembly formally to reject the agreement and, instead, authorized Prime Minister Sadiq al-Mahdi to negotiate with the SPLM/SPLA in light of all the previous initiatives and agreements. The DUP withdrew from the coalition with the Umma, which then formed a coalition government with the NIF and committed itself to the application of the *sharia*. Prospects for peace became even more remote as a result.

In February 1989, the military stepped in by giving the prime minister an ultimatum to adopt the agreement between the SPLM/SPLA and the DUP as a basis for negotiation or to equip the army to fight more effectively. The implication was that the military would take over if the prime minister failed to meet their demands. Sadiq eventually accepted the military directive, which led to the withdrawal of the NIF from the coalition. The Umma Party then entered into another coalition with the DUP and began a dialogue with the SPLM/SPLA on the basis of the earlier agreement with the DUP, but there was reason to believe that the prime minister was ambivalent about the terms of the agreement, which may have been why he left the leadership of the DUP in charge of the peace process. Indeed, while seeming progress was being made, it was doubtful that peace would be forthcoming through the process. Exchanges of statements with the military still indicated a precarious mutual accommodation that could not be relied upon to last. As a result, when the coup took place on 30 June, in the name of national salvation, most observers were not surprised. What was surprising was that it was not the leadership of the army, but a group of previously unknown, relatively young officers of middle rank who took over.

Although the regime is by no means monolithic, its declared policies and pattern of dismissals and appointments across the board indicate a clear promotion of the Islamic trend. The rise in "Islamic power," which this new trend implies, should perhaps not be surprising given the general upsurge of "Islamic fundamentalism" around the world. Within the Sudanese political context, however, there is considerable debate on whether this is real or only apparent. Some people argue that the Muslim Brotherhood and the NIF represent a small, well-organized, and generously funded group that is more enigmatic than it is reflective of the Sudanese Muslim community and its political aspirations. The NIF's influence, however, has grown with its financial resources, which were consolidated during the period of Numayri's alliance with the Muslim Brotherhood toward the latter part of his regime.

Foundations of the Revolutionary Trend

Whatever the role of the NIF in the recent military coup, the rising profile of the Islamic trend in all its various forms as a political force that can influence national politics in a significant way, and of the SPLM/SPLA as its counterforce throughout the country, reflects the development of two important revolutionary patterns from the north and the south. To appreciate the roots of these trends, the point made earlier about the conservatism of Sudanese society should be recalled. In the north, conservatism follows Arab Islamic lines while in the south it follows along indigenous African lines. In both, the society is largely dominated by family or kinship ties and an ancestrally oriented lineage system that stratifies people according to descent, age, and gender. Leaders tend to be from politically and religiously dominant families, men dominate over women, and youth must show filial piety to their fathers and elders.

The northern Muslim community is, as one British observer put it, "A society in which young men are seen and not heard, in which a grey-haired son did not take a seat in front of his father, and abstained from lighting a cigarette when travelling in company with his elder brother."[15] In the south, however, lineage-based political and social structures were qualified, until the impact of recent changes, by an age-set system that ensured institutionalized generational competition, balances, and complementarity. While the elders engaged in the orderly discussion of public affairs and the peaceful settlement of disputes, youth warrior age sets found their status and dignity in warfare and other activities associated with physical vitality, courage, and resilience. As features of organized group action, these activities could be carried out in open challenge to the elders, who accepted the defiance ambivalently as an exaggeration of what was otherwise a necessary military service and a source of pride and dignity among their youth.

These behavior patterns have been affected in contrasting ways by the various systems of government that have ruled Sudan in modern times. The conservatism of the Muslim north was reinvigorated in a fundamentalist way by the mahdist revolution of 1885 which ousted the Turco-Egyptian administration that had ruled the country since 1821. When joint Anglo-Egyptian forces reconquered Sudan in 1898 and established a condominium administration, they found it prudent to recognize, respect, and reinforce the Arab-Islamic cultural identity, values, and institutions of the north to avoid any provocations that might incite a revival of rebellion. State formation and modernization along Western lines were therefore constrained by these cultural considerations. One British governor general even described the Anglo-Egyptian Condominium government as Islamic.[16] The conservatism of northern society prevailed even as it was subtly undermined by the undercurrents of the educational system and the "modernization" process from the West. Because self-assertiveness against family elders, in particular the patriarch, is ruled out, educated northern youth tended to challenge society politically through the ideological tools of communism and the Muslim Brotherhood. Both were radical in opposite ways and both represented well-conceived ideological and political systems that transcended their local frameworks and, therefore, could be conceptually removed from the domestic context and its inherent tensions and constraints. Furthermore, they offered opportunities for widening associations and loyalties beyond the confines of traditional kinship ties.

During the 1950s and 1960s, most northern youth in secondary schools and institutions of higher learning were members of one of these two ideological and political camps, with the Democratic Front—the umbrella organization of the Communist Party—having a slight numerical and organizational advantage over the Muslim Brotherhood. Opposition to virtually all governments was then a conspicuous feature of student politics in Sudan, and it was well known that after they graduated and joined the establishment, most northerners would abandon their earlier affiliation with these two extremes. Yet, ironically, although locally motivated, they were among the most powerful and effective ideological movements in the African and Arab worlds.

In 1971, following an abortive coup against Numayri masterminded by the Communist Party, the regime clamped down on the communists and their leftist sympathizers, virtually eliminating them from the Sudanese political scene. That left the Muslim Brotherhood the only political force challenging the traditional parties. Their position became even more pronounced when Numayri, in his move toward Islam, allowed them to be the only politically active party. Even though the Communist Party was reactivated with the return of political parties following Numayri's overthrow, it has not been able to rival the Muslim Brotherhood, especially under its new organization, the NIF.

Because the National Islamic Front tends to attract the educated youth, it enjoys an intellectual appeal that supercedes the sectarian basis of influence among the traditional political parties—the Umma Party, supported by the Mahdi family, and the Democratic Unionist Party, supported by the Mirghani family. These parties are led by educated elites, but because of their traditional orientation, their following among the more enlightened class can logically be expected to weaken, unless they succeed in reversing their sectarian orientation and broaden the basis of their appeal. As the religious foundation of their sectarianism diminishes, the NIF appeal to the religious sentiments of the Muslim constituency is likely to broaden its influence among educated Muslims of sectarian background. This means that as these sectarian parties and the NIF feed on the same religious ground, they are both potential allies and adversaries. Recent political trends have tended to reflect this ambivalence as the NIF has shifted repeatedly from being in the opposition to joining coalition governments with one or both of the leading sectarian parties.

Although ethnic communities in the south were administered through their traditional leaders and protected or preserved to evolve gradually along the lines of their indigenous cultures, the British did not show the same degree of sensitivity, recognition, and deference to the African cultures as they did to the Arab-Islamic civilization of the north. The system of education introduced by Christian missionary societies, and a language combination of vernacular and English, instilled a Western-type value system that undermined traditional cultures among educated youth. Because the state had to maintain neutrality in its dealings with the competing missionary societies, the notion of separation of church and state was accepted as an essential feature of the modern nation-state.

The reaction of educated southern youth to the traditional conservatism of both south and north has been less ambivalent than that of northern youth. For one thing, the process of modernization associated with state formation and Western education has itself been revolutionary among southerners. At the national level, the reaction of educated youth of the south has been expressed through two rebel movements, the first by the SSLM, which aimed at separating the south from the north, and the current one by the SPLM/SPLA, aimed at creating a new Sudan.

In their revolutionary trends, southern youth have made effective use of the warrior tradition associated with the military role of youth. This is reflected, for example, in their method of naming companies and battalions and in their use of traditional-type war songs for morale boosting. What is remarkable is the extent to which the SPLM/SPLA has shifted the southern outlook from one of a minority, struggling for recognition and a degree of autonomy in a marginalized corner of the country, to one of self-assertiveness, pride, and dignity in the struggle for a secular, democratic, and egalitarian Sudan. In this they have met with support from like-minded people in the north, especially from other marginalized areas where the people have been less Arabized or Islamized in an orthodox fashion.

The Prospects for Peace

The question that continues to vex everyone is why Sudan, which desperately needs peace, has failed so dismally, even though the leaders on both sides of the civil war consistently assert their commitment to the peaceful resolution of the conflict, claim to agree on the identification of the issues that divide them, and seem to recognize the steps needed to redress the grievances involved. Certainly, the dominant leaders in the north must realize that as long as one race, culture, or religion is favored as the basis of national identity and participation in the political and economic life of the country, there can be no equality, and without at least the legal framework for equality, there can be no peace.[17] The leadership of the SPLM/SPLA must also recognize that their postulated goal of fundamentally restructuring power to create a new Sudan threatens the very core of the Arab-Islamic identity and value system that have so far dominated the country. If leaders are aware of these factors from each other's perspective and want the country to remain united, then why do they not make the necessary compromises based on mutual accommodation? The answer may lie in the difficulties associated with compromise.

If one takes the point of view of the SPLM/SPLA and, indeed, of the south in general, it is not far-fetched to argue that the history of south-north relations has convinced them that the wielders of power at the center, and, indeed, most northerners, are not going to heed the message of southern grievances unless and until their cause is demonstrated on the battlefield. Whether or not this can be done is a different issue. Despite the SPLM/SPLA's impressive performance in the field, the movement and most of the more politicized southern population believe that the point has not yet been reached when the north will accept the need for radical changes that will lead to the restructuring of the national power process.

On the part of the successive governments in Khartoum, the success of the SPLM/SPLA to any significant degree in achieving its declared objectives—whether through military or political means—would undoubtedly threaten the dominance of the center and the Arab Muslim north. Naturally, except for rare statesmen, it is difficult for any leader in Khartoum to make such a major concession.

Comparable factors may be at work with respect to the issue of unity and separation. With the prolongation and intensification of the conflict, both the forces of unity and separatism have been paradoxically strengthened. Although the leadership of the SPLM/SPLA has consistently stood for the unity of the country, and their commitment appears to be strategic, there is little doubt that separatism evokes deep-rooted sympathy if not open support in southern circles. The north, too, has become less certain about the value of unity under the conditions of chronic military confrontation and its political, economic, and moral impact on the nation as a whole.

Perhaps the only encouraging development is that both parties appear to have accepted the principle of a federal constitution. The critical issue that remains to be resolved is whether Islamic law should apply on the federal level and the non-Muslim states be allowed to opt out, which is the government's position, or the federal constitution be secular and any Muslim state wishing to do so be allowed to enact Islamic laws within its own state jurisdiction, which would presumably be more acceptable to the SPLM/SPLA.

It is safe to predict that, sooner or later, Sudan will find a solution to this problem, even if it amounts only to another interlude of peace. The question is how much more destruction it will take before peace can be achieved and under which government and which leadership this will be accomplished. It is a choice between making history in a positive sense or becoming a victim of history.

NOTES

1. Indeed, the main problem that confronted the Sudanese on independence was the role of religion in the affairs of the state. In 1956, Hasan Muddathir, the grand *qadi* of Sudan—the head of the Muslim division of the legal system—in his memorandum to the constituent assembly, argued that, "In an Islamic country like the Sudan, the social organization of which has been built upon Arab customs and Islamic ways and of which the majority are Moslems, it is essential that the general principles of the Constitution of such a country should be derived from the principles of Islam; and, consequently, the laws governing its people should be enacted from the principles of an Islamic Constitution and in accordance with Islamic ideals out of which such a community has been shaped." "A Memorandum for the Enactment of a Sudan Constitution Derived from the Principles of Islam," as quoted in F. M. Deng, *Dynamics of Identification: A Basis for National Integration in the Sudan* (Khartoum: Khartoum University Press, 1973), p. 22.

2. For a background on the conflict and a history of the first phase of the war, see Mohamed Omer Beshir, *The Southern Sudan: Background to Conflict* (London: C. Hurst and Company, 1968, republished by Khartoum University Press, 1979). See also Dunstan M. Wai, *The Southern Sudan: A Problem of National Integration* (London: Frank Cass, 1973) and idem., *The African-Arab Conflict in the Sudan* (New York and London: Africana Publishing Company, 1981). For a southern point of view, see William Deng and Joseph Oduho, *The Problem of the Southern Sudan* (Oxford: Institute of Race Relations, 1962),

and Oliver Albino, *The Sudan: A Southern Viewpoint* (Guildford and London: Billing & Sons, Ltd., 1970).

3. For a detailed account of the Addis Ababa agreement, see Ministry of Foreign Affairs, *Peace and Unity in the Sudan: An African Achievement* (Khartoum: Khartoum University Press, 1973).

4. For the reasons leading to the resumption of hostilities and what the SPLM/SPLA stands for, see Mansour Khalid, ed., *John Garang Speaks* (London and New York: KPI Ltd., 1987). See also, Bona Malwal, *A Second Challenge to Nationhood* (New York: Thornton Books, 1985).

5. In the Sudan, unlike other African countries with a Muslim population, Islam is closely associated with Arab language, culture, and race, perhaps because of the historical association with the Arab world and in particular with Egypt.

6. According to H. A. McMichael, "All these people [Northern Sudanese] are Mohamedans and have Arab blood in their veins, but racial characteristics derived from non-Arab ancestors have survived very persistently." *A History of the Arabs in the Sudan, vol. I* (Tuckahoe, NY: De Graff, 1967), p. 13. See also, A. J. Arkell, *A History of the Arabs* (London: London University Press, 1955), in which he states, "There is in the Sudan of course every conceivable degree of admixture between the Brown and the Negro races," p. 22.

7. The Umma Party, for instance, whose support is overwhelmingly from the rural, more neglected regions of the western Sudan, has recently begun to experience complaints by the representatives of those regions within the party.

8. See, Talal Asad, *The Kababish Arabs* (London: C. Hurst and Company, 1970) and Ian Cunnison, *Baggara Arabs* (Oxford: Clarendon Press, 1966).

9. This was tragically demonstrated by the execution of the leader of the Republican Brothers, Mahmud Muhammad Taha by the Numayri regime on January 18, 1985, through the application of the September Laws, which he had denounced as discriminatory to the non-Muslim and to women and as incompatible with the ideals of Islam and the moral standards of the international community.

10. According to K. D. D. Henderson, "By 1957 it seems to have been generally accepted in the North that the confidence of the Southern intelligentsia had been lost. It could only be recovered by concessions which the North was not prepared to make. The solution must have appeared to lie in taking a leaf from the book of the old government and putting Southern policy into reverse, as it were. The influence of the existing intelligentsia could be weakened by cutting away its feeder system, the mission schools from which it was recruited. Substitute a system of Islamic education uniform with that of the North and within a decade you will have built up a new pro-Northern Arabicized student body to replace the now discredited leaders of the nineteen-forties." *The Sudan Republic* (London: Ernest Benn Ltd., 1965), p. 183.

11. For an account of the return of slavery, later supported by the media, see Ushari Ahmed Mahmud and Suleyman Ali Baldo, *Al-Diein Massacre: Slavery in the Sudan* (Khartoum: Initially published privately by the authors and subsequently reproduced by the Sudan Relief and Rehabilitation Association in London, 1987).

12. For the reaction of the SPLM/SPLA, see John Garang de Mabior, "Statement to the Sudanese People on the Current Situation in the Sudan," (General Headquarters, SPLM/SPLA, August 10, 1989).

13. For the official report on the conference, see The Steering Committee for National Dialogue on Peace Issues, "Final Report and Recommendations," Khartoum, 1989.

14. For the texts of the Koka Dam declaration and the SPLM/SPLA-DUP agreement, see annexes in Abdel Ghaffar M. Ahmed and Gunnar M. Sorbø, eds., *Management of the Crisis in the Sudan*, Proceedings of the Bergen Forum, February 23–24, 1989, Center for Development Studies, University of Bergen, 1989.

15. K. D. D. Henderson, *The Sudan Republic*, p. 75.

16. In a speech delivered to a northern Sudanese audience in 1914 the governor general proudly announced, "God is my witness. We have brought the Holy Places within a few days' journey of Khartoum. We have subsidized and assisted the men of religion. We have built and given assistance for the building of mosques all over the country. Finally, the Kadis and others have received a free and thorough education in the Koran and in the tenets of the Mohamedan Religion." As quoted in J. Spencer Trimingham, *Christian Approach to Islam in the Sudan* (London: Oxford University Press, 1948), p. 26.

17. At a Washington seminar on the problems and prospects of peace and unity in the Sudan, held at the Wilson Center for International Scholars in February 1987, Islamic scholar Abdullahi A. An-Na'im stated that, "Common perceptions of Shari'a, accepted by all factions of the political leadership of the Northern Sudan, in fact violate the fundamental rights of non-Muslims and individuals in general. Shari'a does not conceive of the permanent residence of non-believers within an Islamic state. At best, non-believers may be allowed to stay under the terms of a special compact which extremely restricts their civil and political rights. Believers who are not Muslims, mainly Jews and Christians, are allowed partial citizenship under Shari'a. In exchange for being allowed to conduct their private affairs in accordance with their beliefs and customs while enjoying Muslim protection, these peoples, known in Shari'a as *dhimmis*, must pay a special tax, *jizia*, and are disqualified from holding any position of authority over Muslims. As such, dhimmis are disqualified from holding general executive or judicial office in their own country." An-Na'im's paper, "On Sudanese Identities," appears in Francis Deng and Prosser Gifford, eds., *The Search for Peace and Unity in the Sudan* (Washington: The Wilson

Center Press, 1987). See also Martin Daly, "Islam, Secularism, and Ethnic Identity in the Sudan," in Gustavo Benavides and M. W. Daly, eds., *Religion and Political Power* (New York: State University of New York, 1989), pp. 83–97. For the contrasting philosophy of the Republican Brothers and more specifically, of their late leader, Mahmud Muhammad Taha, see his *Second Message of Islam*, trans. Abdullahi Ahmed An-Na'im, (Syracuse University Press, 1987).

Sudan's Foreign Policy

IN SEARCH OF ARMS, AID, AND ALLIES

Ann Mosely Lesch

Sudan's foreign-policy options are constrained severely by its geo-strategic location and complex socio-economic composition. Both constraints promote foreign interference and exacerbate inherent political tensions. Governments have crafted different strategies to maximize Khartoum's bargaining power in relation to its neighbors and to concerned global powers. Some regimes have sought to promote a nonaligned posture that would widen diplomatic options and flexibility, while others have cultivated political alignments that would afford them protection from regional rivals. Each strategy has served Sudanese needs to some degree, but has also created additional complications. The difficulty of crafting a coherent and effective foreign policy was demonstrated starkly in the 1980s, when Sudan was ruled by four different governments and suffered a sharp escalation in civil strife. The search for arms, aid, and allies led each government in a different diplomatic direction. None proved fruitful so long as the government failed to come to grips with internal political and economic problems. Looking for foreign props for their power or using another state as a scapegoat underlined the weakness of these regimes and the incoherence of their strategies, and tended to expose the country to further external pressure rather than to promote its independence.

Geo-Strategic Constraints

The location of Sudan, its ethnic composition, and its economic difficulties all affect its foreign-policy options.[1] Sudan lies astride the Nile, the headwaters of which are located in Ethiopia and Uganda. The Blue Nile and White Nile converge at Khartoum and then flow through Egypt, providing that country's sole source of water for agriculture, hydroelectric power, and basic human needs. Egypt maintains a vigilant concern for access to the river and therefore monitors its use by upstream states, fearing that they will divert essential supplies of water for their own use.

Sudan also borders the Red Sea, a major artery of international trade. Eleven percent of world maritime trade passes through the Suez Canal. Both global and regional powers seek open passage through the Red Sea and fear its embroilment in superpower, Arab-Israeli, inter-Arab, or Ethiopian strife. Sudan's long coastline and proximity to those areas of conflict enhance its strategic importance.

Moreover, Sudan, the largest state in Africa, adjoins eight countries. Lacking the capacity to police its remote desert borders, the country is vulnerable to incursion. Its territory also provides sanctuary for citizens of neighboring countries when famine and warfare force them to flee their homes. Refugees from past conflicts in Zaire and Uganda as well as from current strife in Ethiopia and Chad have found haven in Sudan. Sudanese likewise flee to neighboring territories when they face political or economic hardship at home, and guerrilla forces find haven and bases under the protection of neighboring governments. Egypt, Libya, and Ethiopia, in particular, have used their influence either to prop up regimes in Khartoum or to subvert them. Porous borders facilitate such intervention.

The ethnic complexity of the country also affects its foreign policy. Tribal and linguistic groups straddle borders, sometimes having closer affinity with peoples of neighboring countries than with fellow Sudanese. The Fur look toward Chad, the Beja cross into Ethiopia, the Nubians merge with southern Egyptian residents, and Equatorian peoples have affinities to groups in Zaire, the Central African Republic, Uganda, and Kenya.

Old rivalries with Ethiopian kingdoms, the legacy of Egyptian rule in the 19th century, and the Anglo-Egyptian Condominium's policy of isolating southern districts from the north still impact on attitudes and policies today. Sudanese have close but ambivalent relations with Egypt, recognizing multiple ties and mutual dependence on the Nile but resenting the paternalistic tendencies of Egyptian governments. Relations with Ethiopia, with which Sudan shares a 2000-kilometer border, have been strained. Historical tensions have been compounded by religious, ideological, and ethnic differences and are embodied in mutual efforts at subversion and destabilization.

Broad differences between the Arab and African socio-cultural aspects of Sudan have also played a role in foreign policy. Some Sudanese see their country as a "terra media" linking the Arab and African worlds, whereas others perceive it as being on the fault line dividing the two.[2] The latter seek to link Sudan with either Africa or the Arab world, rather than to promote a multiple identity. At least 40 percent of the population speak Arabic as their home language, and a majority identify themselves culturally as Arab. Some 70 percent are Muslim. Muslim Arabs from the central provinces along the Nile dominate the government as well as economic and educational institutions. They identify with the Arab and Islamic worlds and seek support from those states during periods of strife in the African-oriented south. Rebels in the south and west, in turn, have sought sanctuary and aid from Africa. Internal cleavages are thus reflected in diplomatic orientations, and foreign-policy thrusts reflect back upon and exacerbate domestic conflicts.

Finally, Sudan's economic problems affect its foreign-policy orientation to a significant degree. Its economy is heavily dependent on the outside world. Agricultural exports such as cotton, groundnuts, and meat require stable external markets and are subject to fluctuating prices in the international arena. Sudan relies on imports for all its petroleum and to meet all its heavy industrial and technological needs. The country requires substantial foreign aid to underwrite development projects, reduce the trade deficit, and ensure survival of its people in time of famine. Revenue from exports covers less than half the import bill, even when the latter is stripped to bare essentials. Governments have therefore sought to lessen debt burden by exploring for oil and expanding local industries and agriculture. They have also sought to diversify external sources of aid. But oil exploration has proven hostage to the war in the south, and aid relationships have been constricting. Foreign donors expect to be repaid and also anticipate political dividends. Khartoum's inability to repay donors makes them wary, and political demands breed popular resentment. The crushing cost of prosecuting the war in the south has worsened the government's budgetary crises and exacerbated the tendency to cater politically to whatever global or regional power will supply armaments, petroleum, and cash. That dependency has led to rhetorical emphasis on cold war or Islamic themes that are not fundamental to internal tensions but help to guarantee foreign support. Rhetoric, in turn, sharpens internal politization and reduces prospects for resolving domestic conflict.

The strategic and socio-economic realities of Sudan have led governments down internally inconsistent—indeed, self-contradictory— paths. The results have often complicated the country's problems rather than ameliorated them. Nearly all regimes have stated a preference for a non-aligned foreign policy that would allow them to maintain good relations with regional and global partners. Nonetheless, the difficulty of satisfying all partners simultaneously and the risk that those partners will manipulate Khartoum's weakness for their own interests have tended to lead governments into forming alliances or at least special relationships with stronger countries that might protect Sudan. Lacking a strong and coherent Sudanese identity, the country is exposed to and buffeted by external influences. Thus, internal contradictions and geo-strategic weakness feed upon and compound each other. No government has broken out of that vicious circle and found a way to secure Sudanese internal tranquility and external stability.

Numayri's Axis with the West

When Jaafar Muhammad al-Numayri and his army colleagues seized power in May 1969, they supported a pan-Arab approach that endeared them to radical secular regimes in Egypt and Libya. They distanced the Sudan from the conservative monarchies of the Arabian peninsula and Ethiopia.[3] Numayri also welcomed support from the Sudanese Communist Party and received arms from the Soviet Union. Within three years, however, he shifted course. The abortive communist coup in July 1971 soured relations with Moscow and reinforced ties with Egypt and Libya, which had helped Numayri to stay in power. Resolution of the 17-year war in the south, with the assistance of the Ethiopian emperor, improved diplomatic prospects in Africa and led to rhetorical emphasis on the mediating role that Khartoum could play between the Arab world and newly independent Africa. Numayri's effort to expand agriculture and establish industries caused a turn to the West for development assistance and technology, as well as to the oil-rich Arabian peninsula. Sudanese officials described their country as the future breadbasket of the Arab world and argued that they needed open borders and good relations in order to flourish economically. Numayri saw little reason to fear his neighbors and every reason to be optimistic about the country's prospects.

The optimism was short-lived. By the early 1980s, Sudan was aligned closely with the United States and Egypt, locked in hostility with Libya and Ethiopia, and heavily indebted to the West and to conservative Arab states. Internal tensions had escalated as Numayri backed away from his accord with the south and embraced Islamic law. Cold war and regional rivalries also forced Numayri to take sides. He used the resulting alignment with Washington and Cairo to his advantage, but paid a steep price for those ties. Moreover, when fighting resumed in the south in 1983, neither ally agreed to finance or support a military solution. Numayri was isolated externally as well as internally by the time he fell from power in April 1985.

US-Sudanese relations had begun to warm in late 1974, when Haile Selassie was overthrown by a pro-Soviet military regime in Ethiopia, thereby ending the long-term American civilian and military presence there. Sudan became the preferred forward-base for Washington: adjoining Ethiopia and the Red Sea, near the Arabian oilfields, and countering an increasingly antagonistic Mu'ammar Qaddafi in Libya. Sudan also served as a strategic rear for Egypt, in part because Numayri supported Egypt's treaty with Israel and cooperated against Libya. The fall of the Shah of Iran in January 1979 and the subsequent hostage crisis in Tehran also galvanized Washington's search for alternative bases and listening posts. The Soviet Union's invasion of Afghanistan in December 1979 and its growing presence in not only Ethiopia but also south Yemen reinforced US fear of Soviet domination of the petroleum-transport lanes and penetration of the Horn of Africa.

Numayri welcomed attention from Washington, especially as it brought vastly increased levels of armament and economic aid to the country. He accorded the US special air and naval rights and held joint military maneuvers with American and Egyptian forces in 1981 and 1983. On frequent visits to Washington, Numayri stressed the role Sudan could play as a bulwark against communism and in support of Egypt. In return, he received the largest military and economic aid package of any African country aside from Egypt.

Numayri also deepened relations with Cairo. In 1974 he signed an "integration pact" with Egypt and reached an accord on construction of the Jonglei Canal. That 300-kilometer waterway would drain a fifth of the Sudd marshes in the south, thereby reducing evaporation from the White Nile and increasing the water available for both countries. Egypt was to cover half the construction costs and gain half the increased flow. In 1976 Anwar al-Sadat helped Numayri repel a broad-based coup by civilian political forces exiled in Libya. Moreover, Numayri remained loyal to Sadat in 1979 when virtually all Arab governments broke diplomatic ties in the wake of the Egyptian-Israeli peace treaty. He cemented relations in 1982, shortly after Sadat's assassination, by promulgating a comprehensive "integration charter" and promoting the Nile Valley Parliament as a symbol of unity between the two countries.

Economically, alignment with the US resulted in ample loans from the International Monetary Fund (IMF), the World Bank, and several Arab funds. Bilateral deals were made with European and Arab governments. Those underwrote expansion of cotton and groundnut projects, the construction of sugar-processing plants and other light industries, rehabilitation of aging railway lines, and expansion of the road network. When Chevron struck oil in Muglad and Bentiu in 1979, Sudanese officials hoped to achieve self-sufficiency in energy and to gain funds to promote substantial development throughout the country.

Alignment with the US and Egypt, however, had a price. Numayri argued that he served as a bulwark against communism in northeast Africa, but he discovered that tying himself to Washington increased the hostility of neighbors. The tripartite agreement of Libya, Ethiopia, and south Yemen in 1981 appeared to encircle Sudan and exposed its vulnerability. Moreover, the Libyan invasion of Chad placed direct pressure on the western province of Darfur. Libyan troops made incursions across the border, Chadian forces crossed the invisible boundary, and Libyan bombers strafed Sudanese villages. Numayri could not police and protect his western border, and relied on American AWACs and Egyptian air defenses for surveillance.

Meanwhile, Sudan provided sanctuary for Eritrean and Tigrean civilians fleeing the civil war in Ethiopia. Numayri allowed their political movements to open offices in Khartoum, operate informally in the refugee camps near the border, and staff medical clinics that aided the war-wounded. He closed his eyes to the unloading of military provisions at the derelict port of Suakin and their transport by truck to Eritrea. Those moves, however, angered the government in Addis Ababa and risked its undertaking military and political reprisals against Khartoum. The Ethiopian government was also angered by Egyptian-Sudanese accords for developing the Nile, which Addis Ababa felt ignored its interests. With over 80 percent of the waters of the main Nile originating in the Ethiopian highlands, Mengistu Haile Mariam could threaten to construct dams for irrigation and hydroelectric power that would divert crucial resources from Sudan and Egypt. Moreover, Qaddafi promised to finance such dam construction.[4] In an escalating war of nerves, Sudan's vulnerability to pressure from neighbors was exposed. The overlay of cold-war rhetoric heightened tension, even though neither superpower welcomed a direct confrontation between their client states.

In Sudan itself, Numayri's ties with Washington and Cairo were controversial. Pan-Arab and leftist groups resented the cool relations with the Arab world, the failure to ostracize Egypt, the virtual freeze in contacts with Moscow, and military ties with the US. The outlawed Umma Party, led by Sadiq al-Mahdi, for example, differed with Numayri's policy of confronting Qaddafi; Sadiq had lived in exile in Tripoli in the 1970s, and many of his supporters remained there. The National Islamic Front, chaired by Dr. Hasan al-Turabi, participated in the government but sought positive relations with the Islamic Republic in Iran and criticized Numayri's active support for Baathist Iraq. in its war with Iran. Many opposed plans to integrate with Egypt, fearing that Sudanese interests would be subordinated to Egypt's needs. Southern Sudanese were particularly anxious about the connection with Egypt. As early as 1974 there were riots in Juba when rumors spread that Egyptian peasants would settle along the Jonglei Canal. Integration would reinforce the Arab and Islamic aspects of Sudan, weakening further its African and multi-religious character.

The outbreak of renewed civil war in the south in 1983 exacerbated internal divisions and compounded the regime's external problems. The formation and growth of the Sudan Peoples' Liberation Movement and Army (SPLM/SPLA) were linked to deep-set feelings of political and economic discrimination on the part of non-Arab Sudanese, which crystallized in their opposition to redivision of the south in June 1983 and imposition of Islamic law in September 1983. A wide range of Sudanese were alienated by those measures and were angered by the autocratic behavior of Numayri.[5] Secular and traditional Islamic political movements in Khartoum opposed Numayri; only the National Islamic Front backed his version of Islamic law and called for harsh repression of the SPLM and other dissidents.

Libya and Ethiopia took advantage of the civil strife to escalate their opposition to Numayri. Ethiopia provided territorial sanctuary for the SPLA. Under Colonel John Garang, the SPLM/SPLA opened political offices in Addis Ababa, received training and arms from Ethiopian forces, and broadcast political messages using a powerful radio transmitter in Ethiopia. Libya sent weapons and cash to the SPLM, and Kenya and Uganda provided sanctuary for SPLA forces. Those actions heightened Numayri's sense of encirclement and forced him to rely even more on Egypt and the US. Those governments, in turn, took advantage of his dependency to enhance their economic ties with Khartoum and strengthen their military axis. The US even persuaded Numayri to permit Ethiopian Jews to be airlifted to Israel from their refuge in Sudan in 1984–85, thus violating the official Sudanese boycott of Israel. Nonetheless, Washington and Cairo were increasingly concerned about Numayri's political views and actions. Neither government welcomed a hardline Islamic regime, which reminded Washington of Ayatollah Khomeini's rule in Tehran and made Egypt fear religious subversion. Neither government supported Numayri's effort to confront the SPLA militarily: they recognized the seriousness of southern grievances and criticized Numayri's high-handed measures. They did not want their military assistance to be used to underwrite fighting in the south. But both felt deeply committed to Numayri for his past support, and both still saw him as a bulwark against communist penetration. An American official expressed the sense of frustration in early 1985:

> We're in a no-win situation. If we stick with him, we're accused of supporting an increasingly repressive regime. If we limit support, we will be accused of undermining a longstanding American friend.[6]

Both countries began to distance themselves from Numayri. In February 1985, Washington froze $144 million in economic aid while continuing emergency food and refugee assistance and some military aid. When Vice-President George Bush visited Sudan in March as part of a tour of drought-stricken African countries, he emphasized American friendship with the Sudanese people and pointedly downgraded references to the government itself. Egypt removed air-defense forces from Jebel Aulia, the hydroelectric complex south of Khartoum: that move, perhaps unintentionally, signaled a lessened Egyptian commitment to Numayri, since Egyptian forces had been used in the past to help him retain power.

Numayri was particularly damaged by the harm the civil war caused to the economy. After threats and harassment by rebel forces, the French company digging the Jonglei Canal suspended work in November 1983, and Chevron pulled out of Bentiu in February 1984.[7] Although completion of those projects was vital to the Sudan, Numayri could not protect them. Self-sufficiency in oil was postponed indefinitely, and reclamation of land and channeling of water along the White Nile were halted. In addition to losing future income, Numayri lost investments from abroad and spent millions of dollars to prosecute the war. The last IMF loan, for $187 million, came in February 1983, and the Arab Fund suspended loans in August 1984.[8] Saudi Arabia and other oil-rich countries were suspicious of Numayri's brand of Islamic fundamentalism and were angered by his blatant corruption. Only appeals based on Islamic and Arab solidarity against the allegedly anti-Arab and anti-Muslim SPLM kept those governments from writing him off completely. By the time Numayri lost power in April 1985, the Sudan was $9 billion in debt. Although the debt can be only partly attributed to the civil war, the fighting undoubtedly exacerbated the economic crisis and hampered the government's efforts to obtain support from abroad.

Numayri had emphasized the axis with the US and Egypt in order to reinforce his position at home and bolster his credibility abroad. Instead, the alignment isolated him in the region, sharpened his involvement in global polarization, and augmented subversion by his neighbors. In the end, his allies were alienated by his repressive policy at home. They could not and would not keep him in power in the face of swelling domestic opposition. Although Washington made a last-minute pledge of renewed assistance when Numayri flew to the US in late March 1985, neither the US nor Egypt intervened to keep him in power. An uprising had been launched on the streets of Khartoum when he flew abroad, and it soon gained support from the army. They blocked Numayri's return on April 6, and he remained stranded in Cairo.

The Transitional Government (1985–86)

The Transitional Military Council (TMC) immediately issued communiqués that outlined its stand on key political and economic issues. Communiqué four asserted that the new government would establish a foreign policy based on maintenance of Sudanese territorial integrity, non-interference in the affairs of neighboring countries, and adherence to international and regional accords. That stand concurred with the Charter of Allied National Forces for National Salvation. Those forces had brought together the principal groups opposing Numayri, groups which participated in the largely civilian cabinet formed in late April. The charter stated that Sudan should adopt a policy of "nonalignment with a strong commitment to the Sudan's Arab and African identity and a policy of good-neighborliness."[9]

In practice, this meant disengaging Khartoum from close ties with Washington and Cairo and re-establishing amicable relations with Tripoli, Addis Ababa, and Moscow. The new foreign minister, who had served as ambassador to Nairobi, articulated the transitional government's view that discord with neighbors was largely artificial:

> The previous regime sought to perpetuate disputes with neighboring countries and to create conflicts between Sudan and these countries for no plausible or acceptable reasons. Nimeiri was obsessed with the thought that he was being encircled by some neighboring countries.[10]

The government emphasized that better relations with Libya, Ethiopia, and the Soviet Union would not be at the expense of relations with the US and Egypt but would redress the balance and restore normal relations with all countries. Along those lines, the chairman of the TMC, General Abd al-Rahman Suwar al-Dhahab, held his first diplomatic meeting with the American ambassador. Washington pledged a $40 million loan to purchase oil, promised to accelerate the transport of emergency supplies to famine-stricken areas in the west, and quietly canceled plans for joint military exercises in the summer. Moreover, ministers hastened to Saudi Arabia, which offered 730,000 barrels of oil for each of the next three months and lifted restrictions on development assistance. Egypt also proffered food and medicine for the emergency operation and agreed, in principle, that construction should resume on the Jonglei Canal.

International attention focused, however, on the high-profile restoration of relations with Libya. A delegation from the TMC visited Tripoli in late April and agreed to exchange ambassadors. Soon after,

Libyan staff for a Peoples' Bureau arrived in Khartoum, carrying both light arms and crates of Qaddafi's Green Book. They were disarmed at the airport by disconcerted security personnel. A senior official, Abd al-Salaam Jallud, came on May 4 with a planeload of supporters, who drove around Khartoum in trucks as they cheered for Qaddafi and called for unity between the two countries. Qaddafi himself appeared on an unscheduled visit on May 18, the first head of state to come to Sudan since the uprising. He announced that Libya had ceased funding the SPLM, called for unity, criticized the idea of multiparty democracy, and proclaimed that Husni Mubarak would suffer the same fate as Numayri. The Sudanese government was astonished and dismayed at the Libyan political onslaught. The newly outspoken press criticized Qaddafi for trying to buy their friendship by offering tons of free oil.

The TMC soon discovered that basic internal problems involving the economy and the war in the south were more intractable than they had anticipated, and that conducting a good-neighbor policy was not simple. On the economic front, cotton earnings were only half the normal level as a result of low prices on the world market and blight caused by rust and pests that reduced the quantity and quality of cotton available. Inflation was nearly 50 percent per annum, remittances from Sudanese working abroad were shrinking, and payments on foreign debt were overdue. The economy required 100,000 tons of petroleum per month in order to function, but no funds were available to pay for that vital fuel. Even though Libya, Saudi Arabia, and Iran provided free oil and several countries resumed bilateral loans, the fundamental budgetary situation was untenable.

In June and July 1985 demonstrators in Khartoum called for resumption of food subsidies and lower fuel prices. The cabinet gave in to public pressure by cutting the prices of fuel, sugar, and bread. But that action contradicted efforts to reach an accord with the IMF, which demanded further belt-tightening by urban consumers and a drastic devaluation of the currency. The minister of finance threatened to resign as a result of the cabinet's action. He followed through on his threat in November, when the government rejected the accord that he had laboriously negotiated with the IMF. Given the government's inability to meet IMF terms by reforming the currency and holding down wages and benefits, and given its incapacity to repay more than $20 million of the $210 million interest owed the IMF, the IMF declared Sudan in default on February 3, 1986.[11] The shock was partly cushioned by grants and loans from bilateral donors, but it highlighted the dilemma facing the transitional authorities. Caught between IMF constraints and public unrest, they responded to the public and postponed formulating a coherent economic strategy. Not until March 1986 did the cabinet convene a national economic conference intended to build a consensus among political forces and trade unions on appropriate policies to tackle the chaotic economy.

The transitional government not only failed to establish economic guidelines but also failed to establish clear political bases for ending the fighting in the south. Indeed, fighting escalated markedly during its year in power. The SPLM insisted that the government cancel the September 1983 decrees and convene a constitutional conference that would not deal solely with the south but restructure the central institutions of the state. The TMC agreed to hold a conference but hesitated to annul Numayri's Islamic laws. Fighting increased in autumn 1985, after the rainy season ended. The SPLA overran several government garrisons and even sent a battalion into the Ingessana Hills, near the Roseires dam on the Blue Nile.

Moreover, the TMC's effort to persuade Ethiopia to end support for the SPLM/SPLA failed completely. Khartoum posted an ambassador in Addis Ababa in the summer, for the first time since 1983, but Mengistu did not reciprocate. TMC hints that Eritrean and Tigrean operations would be restricted if Ethiopia stopped helping the SPLA were ignored by Mengistu, who blandly commented that he was not involved in Sudanese internal affairs. Missions to Moscow failed to persuade Mikhail Gorbachev to induce Mengistu to stop helping the SPLM. The only successful missions involved Kenya and Uganda, whose governments agreed to stop letting their territories be used as SPLA sanctuaries.

In that constrained context, the government heightened its rhetoric against the SPLM and turned to Libya for military support. Suwar al-Dhahab appealed to the West for aid on the grounds that Garang wanted to rule "all Sudan under a Communist system"[12] like Ethiopia's. Simultaneously, Suwar al-Dhahab appealed to the Gulf states, using the argument that Garang sought to impose an African identity upon the country's Muslim Arab majority.[13] Both arguments widened the gap between the government and SPLM. SPLM activists resented being tarred as communist and anti-Arab, and became even more adamant that the government annul the Islamic laws prior to negotiations. Equally importantly, the government tightened its military relationship with Libya. The minister of defense, General Osman Abdullah, signed a military protocol with Libya on July 9, 1985, that committed Tripoli to assist the Sudanese army in transportation, training, equipment, and naval and air defense. Libya also pledged to send petroleum, provide planes to transport food, and dispatch a thousand trucks to Darfur to handle relief distribution. When Washington and Cairo reacted nervously to this protocol, Suwar al-Dhahab minimized its significance. Nonetheless, some 700 Libyans came by truck and air to al-Fasher, the capital of Darfur, apparently to pave the airport and to transport supplies. Moreover, high-level visits to Tripoli in March 1985 led to provision of Tupolev-22 bombers; journalists reported that Libyan pilots flew two bombers in raids across the south that month.[14] The show of force sought to boost military morale, but it deepened antagonism. Even though the government resisted Libyan demands to unite and rejected Qaddafi's public hostility toward Egypt, its desperation to receive support to defeat the SPLA entangled it in an increasingly complex bilateral relationship. That relationship further complicated its relations with other neighbors.

The government of Hissene Habre in Chad was particularly alarmed at the presence of Libyans in Darfur. Relations with Sudan were already tense. Even though Khartoum had recognized Habre's authority and disapproved of Qaddafi's invasion of northern Chad, Habre feared that Libya would infiltrate its soldiers into Sudan and launch a flanking attack against central Chad. Similarly, Egypt opposed the military protocol with Libya, particularly as it was signed just when Khartoum claimed that it opposed any special military relationships. With the integration accords and defense agreement frozen—and with Numayri's political asylum in Cairo causing on-going friction—Mubarak feared that Libya might take advantage of that tension to damage Egyptian security. Cairo tried to manage the problem by signing a new bilateral commercial protocol with Khartoum in February 1986, by airlifting arms and ammunition to Sudan in March, by agreeing to dissolve the integration institutions, and by offering to mediate with Ethiopia and the SPLM. President Mubarak hoped that he would win long-term credit among Sudanese by lowering the profile of the bilateral relationship and seeking to ameliorate the civil strife; then Egypt's essential interests would be guaranteed.

Sudan, however, found itself caught in the mounting US-Libyan crisis. Washington's concern about Sudan's Libyan ties was first expressed in July 1985 when President Ronald Reagan's spokesman deplored the military protocol with Tripoli.[15] In November, the State Department cut back embassy staff in Khartoum and warned Americans not to travel to Sudan since Libyan subversives were operating from the Peoples' Bureau. The TMC criticized as unwarranted the American stance, but quietly expelled several Libyan envoys. Nonetheless, tension boiled over when the US bombed Tripoli and Benghazi on April 15, 1986. In the aftermath of the Sudanese election campaign for the constituent assembly, when political passions ran high, the politicians and public denounced the American raid as an attack on the sovereignty of a fellow Arab state. The uprising against Numayri had aimed, in part, to restore Sudan's national independence. Now the suspicion appeared confirmed that Washington had hegemonic designs on the Middle East. (US diplomats in Khartoum privately decried the air raid on Libya as counterproductive; they indicated that they felt that Washington had let anti-terrorism dominate strategy and had displayed insensitivity to political realities in the region.) When an attempt was made to assassinate an embassy employee on the evening after the air raid, the embassy panicked and abruptly evacuated all dependents, most staff, and many Americans resident in Khartoum and outlying towns.[16] In the final days of the transitional government, Washington appeared to write off Sudan. Khartoum's effort to walk the tight rope between Libya and the US appeared to have failed.

In its year in power, the transitional government found that maintaining a good-neighbor policy was much more complex than anticipated. The fierce antagonisms among its neighbors and the contradictory pressures by external powers made it impossible to please all parties simultaneously. Creditors wanted political payoffs and regional powers rejected Khartoum's concept of pleasing all comers. Moreover, the transitional government failed to tackle economic problems or devise a strategy to resolve the fighting in the south. It fell back on short-term palliatives and sharpened rhetoric in order to gain foreign support. The government was floundering internally and externally when it turned over power to an elected government in late April 1986.

The Elected Government of Sadiq Al-Mahdi (1986–89)

Sadiq al-Mahdi, heir of the Mahdiyya and leader of the Umma Party, became prime minister on May 6, 1986. The Umma won 39 percent of the parliamentary seats in the April elections and led a coalition government with the pro- Egyptian Democratic Unionist Party (DUP). Southern parties also gained token representation in the cabinet.

Sadiq had long criticized Numayri's alignment with Egypt and the US. In May 1979, shortly after Khartoum broke with the Arab consensus against the Egyptian-Israeli treaty, he had commented:

> Sudan's ties with Egypt led it down a predictable path of support for the US and anti-Soviet initiatives in Africa. . . . This committed foreign policy was too inflexible. It invited reprisal from Soviet allies on Sudan's very borders. And by over-identifying with one superpower it . . . restricted Sudan's freedom.[17]

Therefore it was not surprising that Sadiq sought to reinforce and consolidate the good-neighbor policy begun by the transitional government. In his inaugural address to the constituent assembly, he stressed the multi-dimensional character of Sudan: simultaneously Arab, African, and Islamic. He mentioned that relations with Egypt would always be special but that those relations needed to be reformulated in a new framework that would represent the will of both peoples. He stated that the government would sign a "brotherhood charter" with Saudi

Arabia, foster closer relations with Libya, and support a covenant linking all the Nile Valley countries. In interviews, Sadiq stressed that Khartoum would not take the side of one party against another; rather, it would base relations on Sudan's own principles and interests. "We do not accept Libya's view of the US and Egypt, just as we do not accept Egypt's view of Libya and the US view of Libya."[18]

At first Sadiq al-Mahdi tried to follow through on this approach by visiting Moscow in August and Washington in October, traveling to Libya, Saudi Arabia, and Iran, and hosting Qaddafi in Khartoum. The foreign minister, a senior member of the DUP, traveled to Iraq and Egypt, while other ministers went to Uganda and Chad. Sadiq also met Mubarak, Mengistu, and Garang in July at the summit conference of the Organization of African Unity (OAU) in Addis Ababa. Thus he cast a wide net, hoping to attract financial support and to reassure neighbors about his intentions.

Nonetheless, Sadiq al-Mahdi soon discovered that the same contradictions that had complicated diplomacy during the transitional period bedeviled his efforts. His visit to Tehran in December 1986 coincided with an Iranian military breakthrough against Iraq and thus made Iraq and Saudi Arabia fear that Sudan would join Libya and Syria as the only Arab states that endorsed Khomeini's revolutionary drive. Qaddafi's uninvited visit to Khartoum in September 1986 occurred just before Sadiq visited Riyadh and Washington. Moreover, Qaddafi's renewed calls for unity and for subversion against Americans in the Middle East as well as against the Egyptian government were acutely embarrassing; Sadiq had been working to reassure American diplomats that he had restored security to Khartoum and had been endeavoring to improve bilateral relations. Qaddafi's visit also worried President Habre of Chad, who hoped Sadiq would expel Libyan agents from Darfur.[19] Moreover, it irritated Garang, who thought that Sadiq had promised to cancel the military accord with Libya as well as that with Egypt. Some observers worried that Sadiq was beholden politically to Qaddafi, since the latter had provided a haven for the Ansar forces in the 1970s and had helped to fund the Umma Party's election campaign.

Relations with Egypt were particularly tense. Cairo was disappointed that the DUP fared poorly in the parliamentary election and was concerned that Sadiq would remain resentful of Egypt for detaining him in Cairo in 1970 at Numayri's request. Although Sadiq declared, "We have now overcome old sensitivities in our dealings with Egypt,"[20] he was wary of his influential neighbor to the north. After he met Mubarak at the OAU summit, differences became more pronounced. Khartoum pressed ahead with a legal case to extradite Numayri to Sudan to stand trial on political and corruption charges. This irritated Cairo, which insisted that it would never expel anyone who had taken asylum. When Khartoum ended the integration accord, Cairo went a step further and suspended bilateral trade. It also set stringent conditions for renegotiating commercial agreements. Nonetheless, as time passed (and Egypt's apparent hope that DUP would take over the government in Khartoum waned), Egypt resumed economic contact. It could not countenance a complete loss of influence in its strategic rear, particularly if that appeared to benefit Libya. Therefore, Sadiq finally visited Cairo in February 1987, where he signed a Brotherhood Charter and renewed trade talks. Playing off Libya against Egypt appeared to benefit Sudan, at least in the short term.

Nonetheless, the same failure to resolve internal problems that had harmed the transitional government bedeviled its successor. The government appeared to operate on an ad hoc basis without devising serious medium-term economic plans to increase exports, rationalize imports, or reduce the crushing debt. In his address to the United Nations General Assembly in October 1986, Sadiq stated that Sudan would follow the example of such Latin American countries as Peru which linked debt repayment to export earnings and social obligations.[21] He hoped, unrealistically, for a ten-year freeze in debt repayment and the cancellation of payments on some of Numayri's more dubious deals. Iran did cancel the interest payments on its $60 million loan, in line with Islamic principles, but other countries insisted on rescheduling loan payments, and the IMF maintained its freeze on assistance. US aid waned from $500 million for economic and military support in Fiscal Year (FY) 1985 to $125 million in FY 1986 and $70 million in FY 1987. That drop reflected an overall diminution in US assistance to Africa, as well as Washington's assessment that Sudan could not absorb development aid effectively. The government entered into barter deals to obtain oil and commodities, since it lacked hard currency and could no longer obtain commercial loans. Meanwhile, corruption soared and merchants profited from rapidly inflating prices. Government officials were even implicated in siphoning off emergency assistance that was airlifted to Khartoum after the devastating Nile flood in August 1988. Renewed price increases in December 1988 triggered major demonstrations in the capital. By the time the finance minister presented the government's budget to parliament in June 1989, the foreign debt exceeded $14 billion and the projected budget deficit was nearly $3 billion.[22] Since only $1.24 billion in foreign aid could be expected, the shortfall had to be covered by borrowing from the central bank. The minister warned that such a step would launch hyperinflation, with disastrous social and political consequences.

Sadiq's inability to devise a coherent economic strategy and adopt measures to rationalize trade and curb corruption undermined the credibility of his leadership internally and externally. The public viewed the economic situation in 1989 as far worse than it had been four years earlier under Numayri. Foreign creditors held the country at arm's length. The elected government's initial success in attracting funds from donors who hoped to see the parliamentary process succeed could not be maintained for long without some tangible return.

The government also failed to develop a strategy to resolve the fighting in the south. Sadiq seemed buffeted by contradictory forces as he tried to placate contention over how to end the civil war. Sadiq initially announced a three-pronged approach: first, to convene a constitutional conference that would resolve fundamental issues of power-sharing, regional autonomy, and the legal code; second, to build up the armed forces in order to maintain security; and, third, to reach an accord with Ethiopia to stop assistance to the SPLM and persuade it to negotiate. However, Sadiq's meetings with Mengistu and Garang in July 1986 were inconclusive and perhaps counterproductive. They failed to agree on the key issue of replacing the September decrees with a secular code. Moreover, when Sadiq suddenly flew to Libya in early August, the SPLM feared that Libya would become more deeply involved in the fighting and announced that any planes flying in the south were liable to be shot down. When the SPLA then downed a civilian plane near Malakal, Sadiq reacted angrily. He called Garang a terrorist and a puppet of Ethiopia, and he accused Mengistu of seeking to replace Sudan's democratic government with a communist regime.[23] During the autumn, the government augmented its support for Eritrean and Tigrean forces and threatened retaliation against Ethiopia. Nonetheless, Khartoum backed off from a direct assault on Ethiopia; the latter could respond with potentially devastating aerial attacks on Sudanese dams and agricultural projects. Sudan, in fact, was far more vulnerable to Ethiopian raids than Ethiopia would be to any feasible Sudanese strike.

Fighting in the south increased during Sadiq's three years in power. Sadiq himself did not undertake any serious effort to negotiate. When the SPLA seized two towns in the province of Blue Nile in November 1987 and overran Kapoeta in eastern Equatoria the next month, the government accused Ethiopia of direct involvement in the fighting. Sadiq began to talk of "African hordes" about to overrun the north. Such rhetoric won him pledges of military support from Libya, Algeria, and Tunisia, intended to ward off alleged Ethiopian aggression. He relied on direct Libyan military air support to help recapture the two Blue Nile towns. By February 1988 Tripoli had provided more than half of all the military aid received by Khartoum.[24]

Meanwhile, the National Islamic Front (NIF) joined the cabinet in May 1988, a move that signaled a further hardening in the government's position on negotiations with the SPLM. Nonetheless, the DUP pursued an independent set of contacts with the SPLM, supported diplomatically by Egypt. Those contacts culminated in an accord in November 1988 between DUP leader Muhammad Osman al-Mirghani and John Garang.[25] The accord outlined a mutual agreement to freeze Islamic laws, convene a constitutional conference, and simultaneously institute a cease-fire and a lifting of emergency law. The NIF immediately denounced the accord, and Sadiq insisted that negotiations remain under his personal control, even though he had not fostered negotiations. Sadiq also delayed implementing the preconditions integral to the accord, thereby prompting the DUP to pull out of the government in December. Sadiq formed a narrow coalition with the NIF, which demanded an acceleration of the military effort in the south. That approach proved disastrous. A dozen southern garrison towns fell to the SPLA in the next two months. Those losses, coupled with the breakdown of talks with the SPLM, forced the hand of the military officers.

In February 1989, the high command of the armed forces issued an ultimatum: the government must either provide the arms necessary to fight the war to the finish or negotiate seriously with the SPLM. In the ensuing constitutional crisis, Sadiq was compelled to exclude the NIF from the government and form a broad-based coalition that would pursue peace efforts. The parliament took actions that met the DUP-SPLM preconditions, including ending the state of emergency. On May 1 the SPLA declared a cease-fire for the month of Ramadan. Moreover, the foreign minister headed an official delegation to Addis Ababa on June 10 that met with the SPLM and laid the groundwork for a substantive session scheduled for July 4 and the long-awaited constitutional conference in September. Sadiq was still reluctant to endorse the accord, however, and he continued to look to Libya for alternative support. Although he initialed the suspension of Islamic law on June 29 and scheduled a cabinet meeting on June 30 to ratify the suspension, he also planned to fly to Tripoli on July 1. The military coup d'état on June 30 overthrew the government and aborted those complex maneuvers.

International Isolation under Bashir

The coup engineered by Brigadier Omar Hassan Ahmad al-Bashir was initially greeted with relief by those Sudanese who were exasperated by the vacillating, incompetent government of Sadiq al-Mahdi. Some thought the takeover was led by the same senior officers who had issued the ultimatum in February and who wanted to finalize negotiations with the SPLM. Others suggested that Egypt backed the coup in order to reinstate Numayri. Within days, however, the middle-rank officers who formed the junta denied that they supported Numayri and abruptly dismissed the senior officers. Instead, their ties with NIF became evident. NIF had a strong incentive to act at that time, since it might be the last opportunity to foil negotiations with the SPLM and prevent the annulling of Numayri's Islamic decrees. Bashir explicitly renounced the DUP-SPLM accord as the basis for negotiations and pressed for the military defeat of the SPLM. His only hints at a compromise involved either letting the south secede or exempting non-Muslim provinces from a few Islamic laws.

In addition to adopting a tough stance toward the civil strife, the junta imposed a strict state of emergency throughout the country. That included suspending the constitution, closing the parliament, and banning political parties, trade unions, and newspapers. Only Islamic societies were permitted to function. Large numbers of politicians, union activists, and journalists were swept into prison. The banned groups tried to undermine the junta by articulating a National Democratic Alliance Charter on October 21, 1989, which called for canceling Islamic laws and completing the peace accord with the SPLM. The Charter espoused a nonviolent popular campaign to remove Bashir from power. Doctors began a strike in November, signaling the first phase of civil disobedience. The junta immediately arrested many doctors, and then engineers; the planned execution of a prominent doctor was stayed only after Mubarak flew to Khartoum to make a personal appeal to Bashir. But Bashir went ahead with large-scale purges of the civil service, armed forces, police, and judiciary in order to weed out opponents of the NIF. Moreover, NIF detained and tortured opponents in secret houses, separate from the prison system, and the government executed 28 officers in April 1990 after an alleged coup attempt.

The severe political crackdown alienated Sudan's traditional supporters. Egypt criticized the detention of DUP leaders, Libya called for the release of Sadiq al-Mahdi, and Iraq decried the arrest of Baathists. The Gulf states were wary of the Islamist influence to their east, fearing the establishment of another activist Islamic state. Qaddafi, while welcoming the possibility of union with Sudan, sharply criticized the Islamists for mixing religion and politics and for alienating the non-Muslim communities.[26] Bashir received some arms and oil from Iran—which had already purchased Chinese weapons on Sadiq's behalf—by appealing to pan-Islam. Efforts were made to gain Arab funds by arguing that the restoration of Israeli-Ethiopian diplomatic relations in November 1989 meant that Israel would have an offensive base on the Red Sea and would assist the SPLA, but the skeptical Arab rulers were not convinced. By summer 1990, the regime's weapons and oil supplies came from only Iraq and Libya. Both expected political dividends.

Iraq's dividend came in August, when Bashir abstained on Arab League resolutions denouncing the Iraqi invasion of Kuwait. Sudanese officials also organized pro-Iraqi demonstrations in Khartoum and supported Saddam Hussain's denunciations of the oil-rich Arabs. There were even reports that Iraqi missiles, stationed in northern Sudan, were targeted at Egypt's Aswan Dam and Saudi Arabia's Red Sea ports. Moreover, Egypt charged that Sudan was training Egyptian dissidents affiliated to the militant Jihad group; the mysterious bombing of the alleged training camp was widely attributed to the Egyptian air force.[27] The Saudi government expressed its concern by beginning to press the Faisal Islamic Bank and Baraka Bank, in whose Sudanese branches the NIF had a dominant influence, to close down their operations in Sudan. Khartoum's isolation was thus deepened by the government's expressed sympathy for Iraq. Moreover, Iraq could not provide arms and oil to Sudan once the international embargo had eliminated its exports and the build-up of forces on its border had necessitated its husbanding military hardware at home. The tie with Iraq proved a liability rather than an asset.

Libya's dividend was far more substantial. Libya had continued its air support for the Sudanese forces fighting in the south, begun three years earlier. In March 1990 Khartoum and Tripoli signed a Charter of Integration that provided for coordination between their security and military forces and for joint efforts for the "dissemination of the Arabic language and Arab culture."[28] Although Qaddafi criticized the politicization of Islam in Khartoum, he embraced the Arabization of the non-Arab peoples there. Moreover, by the summer, the Libyan presence in the western province of Darfur was so substantial that some argued that the government had virtually abdicated its authority in that strategic area. Moreover, Darfur became a battleground between Chadian forces and dissidents in a confrontation fought at the expense of the Fur villagers. For Qaddafi, Darfur provided a vital sanctuary in his renewed effort to oust Hissene Habre from Chad and to find a Chadian ruler who would accept Libyan patronage as well as Libyan paramountcy in the Aozou Strip. Libyan-supported Idris Deby, who had taken sanctuary in northern Darfur in April 1989, launched an invasion of Chad in March 1990. That effort culminated in the fall of Habre's regime in December 1990, as Deby's forces rolled into Ndjamena in Libyan armored vehicles. American and French preoccupation with the crisis in the Gulf—and West African preoccupation with the civil war in Liberia—significantly facilitated Libya's swift *fait accompli*. But the Sudanese sanctuary was also critical to its success. Having achieved his major strategic objective, Qaddafi's interest in and support for Khartoum may well diminish. Nonetheless, Bashir's desperation for Libyan aid is bound to increase. Without that support, he would be totally isolated in the region. Even Iran, which abruptly canceled a planned visit by Bashir in November, has signaled its dissatisfaction by ceasing to send oil to the bankrupt regime.

Western assistance had dried up much earlier. The US Foreign Assistance Appropriations Act required Washington to suspend economic and military aid when the elected government was deposed by force. Only emergency food and refugee assistance could continue. Moreover, US strategic concern for Sudan diminished with the evaporation of the Cold War. Even emergency aid was jeopardized when government forces bombed southern towns where the UN was providing food aid. By fall 1990, the government and donors engaged in a tug of war after the government had suspended all food and medical relief to the south and the US and UN had responded by holding back wheat deliveries. The potentially grave famine caused by poor harvests and the civil war had been exacerbated by the government's selling of 2.5 million tons of grain from its reserve stock to foreign buyers in order to obtain hard currency. Moreover, the government appeared indifferent to the fate of the non-Arab peoples in the south and west. Some Islamists even welcomed the cut-off in western aid on grounds of Muslim purity. But officials were shaken by the IMF's decision in autumn 1990 to issue a formal Declaration of Non-Cooperation. Sudan became one of only two countries world-wide to bear that stigma.

The international isolation of Bashir's government encouraged the opposition forces. The SPLA continued to consolidate its position in the south, but the northern political groups were more divided and demoralized. The public in Khartoum tended to be apathetic toward calls for a renewed uprising, in part because of their fear of the severity of the government's reprisals but also because of their disappointment with the outcome of the 1985 uprising. Nonetheless, the groups backing the Democratic Charter were strengthened in September 1990 by the public support given to them by exiled senior officers and by the diplomatic links established with the SPLM. Leading exile politicians strongly supported Egyptian and Saudi efforts to restore Kuwait's sovereignty. The SPLA even offered a symbolic contingent of 500 soldiers to protect Saudi soil. Opponents of the government undoubtedly hoped that the Arab financial and diplomatic squeeze on Khartoum would undermine NIF and military officers' support for Bashir. Signs of strain became evident when southern officers in the junta expressed their dismay at Bashir's alienation of the exiled government of Kuwait, which had provided significant development assistance in the south. Moreover, some NIF leaders rushed to Saudi Arabia to prevent the pullout of Islamic banks. The public was further demoralized by the cutback in remittances from the Gulf and the risk that Gulf regimes would expel Sudanese employees in retaliation for the government's pro-Iraqi stance. Nonetheless, Bashir clung to power as society and the economy crumbled around him.

Conclusion

The four governments that ruled Khartoum during the 1980s tried to manipulate their diplomacy so as to enhance their authority and expand the country's sovereignty. Numayri thought that a close alliance with the United States and Egypt would serve his interests. The transitional government and Sadiq al-Mahdi thought that a non-aligned policy would help Sudan. Bashir, ruling in self-imposed international isolation, could turn to only Libya for support. Numayri's route exposed the country to increased hostility on the part of powerful neighbors and tied Sudan to one side in the Cold War. The non-aligned approach left Sudan vulnerable to subversion by still-suspicious neighbors and opened it to the accusation that it had shifted regional and global alliances, rather than being genuinely non-aligned. By attempting to be friends with everyone, the governments risked being friends with no one. Indeed, Bashir reaped the fruits of that mistrust and compounded it by his own floundering diplomacy, so that the government became isolated to an unprecedented degree by fall 1990.

Ultimately, foreign policy was hostage to domestic policy. The governments failed to overcome either severe economic problems or accelerating socio-political strife. Their policies accentuated those crises rather than ameliorating them. The increasingly frantic search for arms, aid, and allies led the governments into opportunistic and potentially harmful relationships. So long as no widely legitimate basis for Sudanese political identity was established and so long as the government could not manage its own economy, it would remain open to external influence. With Sudan unable to protect itself from its geostrategic centrality and vulnerability, the vicious circle of domestic instability and external penetration has yet to be broken.

NOTES

1. For an overview of Sudan's geostrategic and ethnic situation, see John Obert Voll and Sarah Potts Voll, *The Sudan: Unity and Diversity in a Multicultural State* (Boulder: Westview, 1985), chapters 1 and 5; and Ann Lesch, "Sudan," in *International Handbook on Race and Race Relations*, Jay A. Sigler, ed. (Westport, Conn.: Greenwood, 1987), pp. 263–67.

2. Mohammed Omer Beshir, *Terramedia* (London and Khartoum: Ithaca, 1982) and contrasting arguments by Francis Mading Deng, Elias N. Wakoson, and Mansour Khalid in *The Search for Peace and Unity in the Sudan*, Francis Deng and Prosser Gifford, eds. (Washington D.C.: The Woodrow Wilson International Center for Scholars, 1987).

3. For general background on Sudanese history and Numayri's regime, see Lesch, "The Fall of Numairi," *UFSI Report*, No. 9 (1985).

4. Dale Whittington and Kingsley E. Haynes, "Nile Water for Whom? Emerging Conflicts in Water Allocation for Agricultural Expansion in Egypt and Sudan," *Agricultural Development in the Middle East*, P. Beaumont and K. McLachlan, eds. (London: John Wiley, 1985), p. 147; and Mansour Khalid, "The Nile Waters: The Case for an Integrated Approach," *The Nile Valley Countries: Continuity and Change*, M. O. Beshir, ed. (Khartoum: Institute of African and Asian Studies, University of Khartoum, 1984), vol. 1, p. 13.

5. Lesch, "Rebellion in the Southern Sudan," *UFSI Report*, No. 8 (1985), pp. 12–13.

6. Lesch, "Fall," p. 13, quoting *The New York Times*, February 17, 1985.

7. Lesch, "Rebellion," pp. 9–10.

8. Lesch, "Fall," p. 5.

9. Lesch, "Transition in the Sudan: Aspirations and Constraints," *UFSI Report*, No. 20 (1985), p. 2.

10. Ibid., p. 10, quoting *al-Sharq al-Awsat*, July 18, 1985.

11. Lesch, "Party Politics in the Sudan," *UFSI Report*, No. 9 (1986), p. 2.

12. *Al-Hawadith*, October 25, 1985, quoted in Lesch, "Confrontation in the Southern Sudan," *The Middle East Journal* 40:3 (Summer 1986), p. 421.

13. *Al-Musawwar*, November 1, 1985, quoted in ibid.

14. *The International Herald Tribune*, March 28 and 29, 1986. The only effort to negotiate during the transitional period was undertaken by the alliance of unions and political parties rather than by the government. It culminated in the meetings and declaration at Koka Dam, Ethiopia, in March 1986. See Lesch, "Confrontation," p. 425, and text of declaration in Deng and Gifford, pp. 24–26.

15. Larry Speakes expressed "grave concern" at the protocol; see Lesch, "Transition," p. 9.

16. Off-the-record interviews in Khartoum, May 1986; see also *The International Herald Tribune*, April 18, 1986, and Lesch, "Party Politics," p. 2.

17. *Guardian*, August 25, 1979, quoted in Mohammed Beshir Hamid, "The Finlandization of Sudan's Foreign Policy: Sudanese-Egyptian Relations since the Camp David Accords," *Journal of Arab Affairs*, 2:2 (Spring 1983), p. 206.

18. *Tadamun*, May 10, 1986.

19. Libya actively supported Habre's opponents living in exile in Darfur, with apparent "tacit acceptance from Sadiq al-Mahdi," according to "Sudan: The Forgotten War in Darfur Flares Again," *News from Africa Watch*, April 6, 1990, p. 4.

20. *Al-Sharq al-Awsat*, June 27, 1986.

21. For discussion of the debt and aid situation, see Lesch, "A View from Khartoum," *Foreign Affairs*, 65:4 (Spring 1987), pp. 818–21, 825.

22. Reuters (Khartoum), June 26, 1989; on deepset corruption and the problems facing the economy, see Jay O'Brien, "Sudan's Killing Fields," *Middle East Report*, No. 161 (November–December 1989), pp. 32–35.

23. Interview with Sadiq al-Mahdi, September 21, 1986; Lesch, "A View,"
pp. 815–16.
24. *The Sudan Times*, January 13, 17, 29, and February 14, 1988.
25. O'Brien, p. 23; on the subsequent political developments, see also *The
Sudan Times*, especially February 13, April 11, May 12 and 28, 1989.
26. *The New York Times*, November 7, 1990. For a brief account of the
coup and its aftermath, see Lesch, "Khartoum Diary," *Middle East Report*,
No. 161 (November–December 1989), pp. 36–38.
27. *Sudan Update*, 2:10 (November 5, 1990), p. 3.
28. Quoted in "Sudan: The Forgotten War in Darfur Flares Again," p. 7.
For an analysis of Deby's defeat of Habre, see *The New York Times*, December
16, 1990, "The Week in Review," p. 2.

Islamization in Sudan

A CRITICAL ASSESSMENT

Carolyn Fluehr-Lobban

Sudan has offered one of the more provocative cases of state-supported Islamization in recent years because of the government's swiftness and readiness to apply the *hudud* punishments after the *sharia* was decreed to be the national law in September 1983. This Islamization, using the coercive apparatus of the state, must be distinguished from the socio-cultural process of conversion to Islam that has been a major part of Sudanese history for the past five centuries.

A number of scholars have described the political context in which Islamization took place,[1] while others have examined the legal effect of this dramatic and far-reaching development.[2] Only a few works have been devoted specifically to southern Sudanese views of Islamization,[3] despite their being a critical dimension to a comprehensive understanding of Sudan. The strongly politicized nature of the north-south divide has made dialogue on the subject infrequent and emotionally charged.

This chapter seeks to examine the political Islamization trend in its more complex character by discussing the deep historical roots of Islamization in northern regions and the fears of Islamization throughout the southern regions. These roots follow a course that is parallel to the formation of Sudan as an entity in the nineteenth century, and it could be readily suggested that the historical examples of the triumph of Islamist forces have been matched by fear and defensive withdrawal of people in the southern regions. Today, the future integrity of Sudan hinges upon the outcome of the current civil war and political debate regarding Islamization. The retention or the abrogation of the sharia is the central issue that divides north and south and prevents an end to the bloodiest and most devastating episode of Sudan's 24 years of protracted civil war.

While journalistic accounts focus on the centrality of racial and religious differences—Arab versus African, or Muslim versus Christian—historical examination of the divisions between north and south reveals deeper patterns of uneven economic opportunity and development. Similarly, the complex role that the nineteenth-century slave trade played in laying the foundation for the fear of the foreigner and the trader from the north, together with a belief that the trade was Muslim and condoned by Islam, laid the basis and set the agenda for north-south suspicions and divisions that have continued to define relations from the nineteenth century to the present. The dichotomy between Islamization—with all of its genuine nationalist and religious aspirations and historical triumphs—and the fear of Islamization—with all of its bitter history of slavery, economic exploitation, and political isolation—yields a more complex, but comprehensible, picture of the origin and the future of the Sudanese national entity.

Nineteenth-Century Foundations:
The Slave Trade, Arabs, and Islam

Although the British outlawed slavery throughout the Empire in 1833, in that same year Britain's Anti-Slavery Society reported that the Turco-Egyptian troops of Muhammad Ali continued to bring out of Sudan 20,000 slaves annually. Often a companion to, or a secondary effect of the ivory trade, the slave hunt—or *ghazwa* as it came to be called—became a common fact of life for the non-Muslim groups south and west of Sennar prior to 1860 and for the people of Bahr al-Ghazal and Darfur after 1865. Originally attracted to the lucrative ivory trade, European and Ottoman merchants recruited private armies from northern groups, such as the Danagla and Shayqiyya, who built fortified trading stations known as *zaribas*, named after their thorn fences.[4] Slaves were required to service these stations and were used as "currency" to pay the merchants' retainers. Raiding of cattle, needed to trade for ivory, and of humans produced interethnic hostility and general societal breakdown by the mid-nineteenth century.

For a period, Europeans dominated the White Nile trade, while the southern Sudan province of Bahr al-Ghazal was penetrated by Egyptian and Syrian traders, using the same zariba system. The role of the *jellaba*, small-scale Muslim traders from the north, expanded with the growth of predatory commerce in the region, and they often acted as agents for wealthier merchants. As the trade "matured," it came to be controlled by a cadre of merchant-princes, one of the most powerful of whom was Al-Zubayr Rahma Mansur, who controlled the trade in Bahr al-Ghazal and the trading routes to Kordofan and Darfur; such was his power that he was appointed by the khedive as provincial governor in 1873. Frequently the ghazwa was the only contact that indigenous people had with foreigners, and it was a terrorizing one. Slavery was conducted for both military and commercial purposes. The Turco-Egyptian armies depended on regular slave raiding, and the demand for domestic slaves in Egypt, the Ottoman Empire, and Arabia was continuous.

With the growing economic interest in Sudan as an extension of Egypt on the part of the British and growing antislavery sentiment at home, a contradiction developed between legitimate commercial interests and activities that might lend support to the condemned slave trade. The contradiction was resolved, in part, by a concerted effort to associate the slave trade with Muslims and with Islam. A literature arose that formulated and articulated this view. In 1840, Sir Thomas Buxton wrote that "Mohamedanism gives the sanction of religion to the slave trade and even enjoins it as a mode of converting the heathen."[5] Others asserted that "slavery is inherent in the religion and social system of Mohamedanism and is congenial to the ideas and customs of Musulman nations."[6] The Anti-Slavery Society readily adopted the view that Islam was a central force behind the slave trade and slavery, a view that fitted nicely with the Christian campaign to suppress the trade and slavery in Sudan.

Today, the reference to "Mohamedanism" is recognized as offensive to Muslims and a fundamental error in the interpretation of Muhammad as divine. The association of slavery with Islam is also erroneous and offensive; while Islam emerged within Arabian society where slavery was already an established institution, the message of Islam stressed manumission as an act of piety and a means of conversion although slavery practiced against non-Muslims continued. Neither in the Quran nor in the Sunna is there countenance for slavery or the slave trade, although there are numerous references to proper conduct regarding slaves as members of households. The spirit of Islam toward the traffic in human beings is conveyed in a tradition ascribed to the Prophet Muhammad, "Sharr al-nas man ba' al-nas" (the wickedest of people are those who sell people).[7]

For their part, the Turco-Egyptians fostered an interpretation of the slave raids—for instance, by calling them *ghazwa*—that would give the impression that they were military campaigns carried out in the name of Islam against the unbelievers. Although most of the Turco-Egyptian rulers in the Nile valley during the nineteenth century responded to British pressure to condemn the trade and officially to attempt to eradicate it, inevitably some rulers, with economic self-interest, claimed that Islam sanctioned slavery.[8]

In nineteenth-century North and East Africa, slavery was practiced in the Muslim north, in Christian Ethiopia, and in the "pagan" south, and Europe was just emerging—rather self-righteously, it might be argued—from four centuries of involvement with slaving, including the Great Atlantic Slave Trade. Later European writers found in the religion and culture of Islam a convenient scapegoat for the continuation of slavery and the slave trade.

The unquestioned assumption that Islam sanctioned slavery created an ideology that justified expanding British interests in Sudan, especially control of the Nile waters, and helped to engender the mood of a Christian crusade to emancipate the region during the Mahdist uprisings and their aftermath. From Omdurman, Mahdist invasions at the frontiers of the religious state were conducted as *jihad* in the west, in the east, and in the south to bring the last vestige of Turco-Egyptian rule in Equatoria under Mahdist control.

Many southern intellectuals and scholars of the southern Sudan contend that the result of this last encounter in the nineteenth century between southern and northern Sudanese was one of bitterness, hatred, and fear of Arabs and Muslims and that this outlook has persisted to the present day in the minds of southern peoples.[9] Oliver Albino writes of an "inborn feeling of dislike and uneasiness in every Southerner about the *mundukuru* or jallaba—Southern names for Northern Sudanese Arabs."[10] Even the most dispassionate southern accounts of the memory of the Mahdiyya recall the khalifa's 13-year rule as "the time when the world was spoiled."[11]

Islamic Purification and Early Sudanese Nationalism

Islamic messianism made a strong appearance in nineteenth-century sudanic Africa, a phenomenon that was reinforced by the pilgrimage tradition.[12] Apart from the breeding ground that the economic and political upheavals of the last century made of Sudan, revivalism has been a persistent and logical feature of Islamic history.[13] In Sudan, Islamic revival and nationalist pride derive from the period of Muhammad Ahmad al-Mahdi. He is referred to by present-day northern Sudanese as "Abu al-Istiqlal," the Father of Independence, for uniting various Sudanese peoples in the northern regions and driving out the alien rulers.[14]

The mahdist state was the first modern Sudanese national entity, governing vast and diverse regions from a central capital at Omdurman, with a centralized legal and political apparatus and its own currency. It was also an Islamic state fashioned to revive the concept and practice of the early Islamic community of Muhammad and his companions. Although the roots of the Islamic revolution, which swept Sudan in the late nineteenth century, are usually traced to the harshness of Turco-Egyptian rule and a nascent Sudanese nationalist response, contemporary scholarship takes a more complex view, one that incorporates internal tensions within the Muslim community at the time, as well as external variables of foreign interests and rule. Peter Holt and Martin Daly argue that the timing of the Sudanese revolt, 60 years after the imposition of Turco-Egyptian rule, was related to the weakening of the empire's hold in Sudan caused by the removal from office of the khedive, Ismail, in 1879 and the British occupation of Egypt in 1882.[15] Gabriel Warburg describes some of the tensions within nineteenth-century Islam in Sudan that played a central role in the dual nature of the Mahdiyya: Islamic purification and revival and nationalist political mobilization.[16]

By the nineteenth century, the sociocultural process of Islamization was in its fourth century in Sudan, with populist Sufi orders the main agents in the spread of Islam. The Sufi brotherhoods, *tariqas*, generally decentralized and egalitarian, were challenged by the imposition of Turco-Egyptian rule, as formal sharia courts, headed by Egyptian *qadis*, were established, and local education became a central government concern. Anticipating antagonism between state-supported and popular Islam, three Egyptian *ulama* were sent with the Turco-Egyptian expeditionary force of 1821 to explain to Sudanese Muslims that their conquest was a legitimate act supported by principles of Islamic government and law.[17] After 1822, increasing numbers of Sudanese ulama were trained formally at al-Azhar University, thereby further undermining local Sufi leaders. The mahdist uprisings of the 1880s, undertaken to rid Sudan of foreign influence, included assaults against Turco-Egyptian state religious personnel and institutions, as well as against its military forces. That conflict between Sudan's indigenous popular Islam and state-supported Islam was resolved by the triumph of the mahdi—the epitome of populist, purifying, revivalist sentiment.

The mahdist state was the only truly anti-imperialist, Islamic republic of its time in Africa, and more than one observer has noted its vanguard role in this respect, while others have drawn parallels to Iran's Islamic revolution. The death of Britain's General Charles Gordon at the hands of the mahdist forces as they overran Khartoum in January 1885 unleashed a furor in England that would not subside until the reconquest of Sudan in 1898. Nearly a century of scholarship, increasingly by Sudanese, has documented the achievements as well as the shortcomings of the independent Sudanese state, which lasted from 1885 until 1898 when an Anglo-Egyptian army retook Khartoum. The mahdist effort to conquer and Islamize the south is still recalled in southern political discourse as a bitter moment in their history. In the context of Sudanese nationalist history, it is important to note that southern Sudanese fought against the Turco-Egyptian presence in the south and, for a brief period, joined forces with the mahdists to expel it from Sudan. In the north, however, the recollection of the mahdi's triumph over the foreign intruder is still capable of mobilizing masses of northern Sudanese; since independence, the great-grandson of the mahdi, Sadiq al-Mahdi, has twice been prime minister, 1967–69 and 1986–89.

Islamization, with its overtly political dimension, has historical roots in Sudan and the rest of Africa beyond today's headlines. In the nineteenth century, the framework of Islamic solidarity produced a bulwark against the penetration of non-Muslim elements—a message that has renewed meaning and importance in contemporary times.

Polarization of Muslim and Non-Muslim in the Twentieth Century

There is little disagreement that during the period of the Anglo-Egyptian Condominium, 1898–1956, relations between north and south did not improve; in fact there was a consciously different and unequal treatment of the regions. From the beginning of British rule, the northern regions were administered separately, with a political policy of indirect rule that incorporated local shaykhs and a separate Sharia Division of the Judiciary that was parallel to the British-derived Civil Division.[18] Although the mahdi's family was initially confined and closely observed for possible insurrectionary activity, by the time of World War I the son of the mahdi, Abd al-Rahman al-Mahdi, rejected the call for jihad by Britain's Ottoman enemies and swore allegiance to the crown. The British developed the rich Gezira land between the Niles for cotton and other commercial crops, while an administrative and transport infrastructure was built to support this key economic activity. Thus, central riverain Sudan developed, while little effort was expended on Darfur or southern Kordofan, the east (excepting the port of Suakin and later Port Sudan), or the southern provinces of Bahr al-Ghazal, Upper Nile, and Equatoria.

As early as 1922, with the Passports and Permits Ordinance, and more clearly from 1933 on, the official policy of the British resulted in the separation of the south from the north through the "Closed

Districts Ordinance," which forbade the use of Arabic and Arab-influenced education, dress, or settlement in the south. An important exception permitted the continued presence of the jellaba merchants—the symbols of the nineteenth-century slave trade. This complex dynamic, as Francis Deng writes, was such that the British tried to give the impression that there was a great difference between the south and the north. "You Northerners," they would say, "are slave traders and you treat the Southerners like *Abeed* [slaves]. Don't call them Abeed! They are slaves no longer. And then they would turn around and say that the Southerners are lazy people and are impervious to progress."[19]

The problem of the south for the British was one of effective political administration, not economic development. Their limited resources required assistance from other sources. Education and health services were largely provided through Christian missionary stations that were established by concession in the south with freedom to proselytize. English, not Arabic, was the language of administration and education. The protection of the region from Islam, and, by extension, the prevention of its penetration into central Africa, made the southern Sudan a kind of bastion of Christian missions.

Islam and Modern Nationalism

Significant nationalist activism began in the 1920s with the rise of the White Flag Society to challenge British occupation; the first demonstrations in Sudanese history were those motivated by political speeches from the mosques.[20] A revolt in Egypt in 1924 inspired mutinies within Egyptian garrisons all over Sudan, but most significantly in Khartoum, where a demonstration was led by a southerner, Ali Abd al-Latif. Others erupted in Wau in Bahr al-Ghazal and Talodi in southern Kordofan. The defeat of the White Flag movement ended its militant confrontation with the British and the possibility of a unified north-south, anti-imperialist front. Thereafter, nationalist sentiments were expressed in Arabic literature and poetry, with references to Arab and Islamic history as well as popular songs.

The Graduates Congress, organized by a group of northern intellectuals—prominent among them, Muhammad Ahmad Mahgoub—gave a framework, a set of terms, and an ideology to continued nationalist aspirations in the 1940s. The national identity of Sudan was conceived of as based upon Islam and Arab culture and founded in African soil and traditions.[21] Yet in their first memorandum to the government, they called for an end to north-south divisions and to Britain's southern policy in Sudan.

The traditionally powerful religious sects became mobilized in the growing nationalist movement. In 1945 the Umma Party—whose name carries a strong reference to the Muslim community—was organized by the mahdist Ansar to give voice to an independent and Islamic future for Sudan. The pro-unionist Khatmiyya *tariqa* also depended upon the common ideology of Arabism and Islam, but its political program supported unity with Egypt. The secular nationalist Communist Party was established in 1946, while the Muslim Brotherhood was founded in 1953 with a clear program for an Islamic state.

The discussions prior to independence in 1956 were dominated by the issue of union or separation of Sudan and Egypt. Concerning the issue of the constitutional make-up of an independent Sudan, virtually all of the key political parties, except for the Communist Party, called for a more central role for Islam than had existed under British rule. Northern politicians dominated the transition to independence, and, again, only the Sudanese Communist Party recognized the seriousness of the southern question and the role that religion should play in the future secular state. A feeling of isolation on the part of southerners from the nationalist political process resulted in resentment and isolation. The post-independence constitution committee, for example, rejected southern requests for federation and called, instead, for a united Islamic Sudan.

Islam and Sudanese Constitutional Development, 1956–1983

After more than five decades of British rule—1898–1956—the political agenda was set to expand the role of Islam in government. The Muslim Brotherhood, through its lobbying group, the Islamic Front for the Constitution, advocated that Sudan should become an Islamic state, basing both constitution and law solely on the Quran and Sunna.

In 1957, a year after independence, the Umma Party and Khatmiyya sect issued a joint statement in which they called for Sudan to develop an Islamic parliamentary republic, with the sharia serving as the sole source of legislation. The first prime minister, Ismail al-Azhari, who ruled from 1956 to 1958, declared that Sudan would be made an Islamic republic from within parliament.[22] The call for an Islamic state did not move beyond the stage of political rhetoric, because in November 1958 the first of Sudan's three military governments—that of General Ibrahim Abbud—took control and held power for the next six years until it was overthrown by a populist revolution in October 1964.

The deep-seated fear among southerners of Islamization and Arabization was accelerated under Abbud's rule whereby official government policy was national integration through the enforced spread of Islamic education and conversion and the promotion of Arabic as the national language. Missionary schools were nationalized, foreign missionaries expelled, and the day of rest changed from Sunday to Friday, provoking resistance and region-wide student strikes in 1960.[23] By 1963, the Anya-Nya guerrilla army was founded, and the first period of civil war began in earnest.

After the 1964 revolution, various unresolved political questions raised at the time of independence were subjected to fresh examination in the light of the new Sudanese democracy. The National Committee to Establish a Constitution—the country was still without a permanent constitution—recommended that the constitution be derived from the principles and spirit of Islam and that the sharia be the basis of all legislation. Meanwhile, the Round Table Conference convened in 1965 to discuss the southern question, and although it advanced the critical dialogue between northern and southern politicians—agreeing to a nonseparatist future for the south—it nevertheless failed to reach agreement on the constitutional issue of the status of the south vis-à-vis federation, regional autonomy, or any other configuration in a unified Sudan.[24]

It was left to the second military ruler, Jaafar al-Numayri—who seized power in 1969—to implement a policy of regional autonomy for the south, and, ultimately, to negotiate the Addis Ababa accords that formally ended the civil war and brought about the integration of southern institutions and leaders into the government and society of the entire Sudan. Freedom of religion was ensured and Arabic became the national language, with English the principal language of the southern region.

The first Permanent Constitution of Sudan was adopted in 1973 during the early years of Numayri's rule. It states that "Islamic law and custom shall be the main sources of legislation; personal matters of non-Muslims shall be governed by their personal laws" (article 9). Under article 16, Islam, Christianity, and "heavenly" religions are equally protected. This latter reference to the protection of the "heavenly" religions of the south, formerly viewed as pagan and therefore potential converts to either of the competing world religions, was considered a victory for southerners—many are neither Christian nor Muslim.

From Peace to War, State-Supported Islamization: 1983 to the Present

Events in 1983 represent a turning point in Sudanese history and epitomize the assertion that Islamization and the fear of Islamic domination are deeply and profoundly related in Sudan. Further, it is also clear that a distinctly anti-Islamist political agenda is the result of the advocacy of an Islamist agenda in Sudan. Two events serve to illustrate this powerful relationship: in May 1983, significant numbers of southern troops mutinied, and the second period of civil war ensued; in September 1983, Numayri decreed that the sharia henceforth would be state law. A contributing factor to the renewal of civil war was southerners' disappointment with the regime's failure to fulfill the Addis Ababa accords, especially regarding economic development and the issue of the discovery of oil in the south that would be refined in and exported from the north. The increased reliance of an ever more isolated Numayri on the political agenda of the Islamic right resulted in the convergence of these two powerful opposing forces in the transforming events of 1983 with which Sudan is now coping and, ultimately, must reconcile.

The specific events leading to Numayri's Islamization through the now infamous "September Laws" have been adequately summarized elsewhere.[25] Upon further reflection, however, what had been viewed as a dramatic new move by Numayri had actually been anticipated by events dating at least to the post-1976 coup attempt that Numayri survived and that resulted in a personal revival of Islam explained in his book, *Why the Islamic Path?* By 1977 a committee to bring Sudanese law into conformity with the sharia had been formed and had drafted various pieces of legislation, including a ban on alcohol and the institution of *zakat*, and the Muslim Brotherhood had taken control of most university student political groups.[26] Legislative attempts to Islamize Sudanese law through the use of democratic means—that is, via the single party, the Sudan Socialist Union's People's Assembly— were less than completely successful because of the strength of the opposition mounted in the assembly, chiefly from its southern constituents. The political estrangement of southern politicians from Numayri over the Islamization issue was already well established by the time southern forces mutinied at Pibor and Bor on May 19, 1983. The 1985 massacre of southern intellectuals in Juba and Wau was widely believed to be the work of the Numayri government to eliminate southern opposition to Islamization.

Having engaged the Sudanese army loyal to Numayri on a number of occasions and having seized foreign hostages, especially those associated with the government-approved development projects—Jonglei Canal and Chevron Oil—the new southern movement's military potential was manifest. Its political agenda was announced with the founding of the Sudan People's Liberation Movement (SPLM) and the Sudan People's Liberation Army (SPLA) on March 3, 1984, whereby the nonseparatist, nationalist, pan-Sudan character of the movement was declared. From the outset, a clear and consistent demand of the SPLM has been the removal of the sharia as state law.

Southern rebels and politicians were not the only groups opposed to the Numayri-imposed Islamization. Northern secular and religious voices—long subdued by the repression under Numayri, beginning largely in 1983—began to criticize the imposition because of the government's undemocratic method of introducing the sharia and for the failure to employ the Islamic method of *shura* (consultation) in its implementation. Sadiq al-Mahdi was arrested shortly after the announcement of the September Laws for his opposition to this move. The judiciary, with its tradition of independence and respect for the rule of law, was reluctant to accept the sweeping changes Islamization meant, and many judges refused to implement mandated changes. Numayri's response—to sack the judges and appoint new ones, often recruits from the ranks of the Muslim Brotherhood—exposed the bias of the "new order." In response, Numayri created his own "Courts of Prompt Justice," whose excesses in applying the harsh hudud penalties, with amputations for relatively simple theft and whippings for alcohol offenses, became notorious. These measures amounted to a reign of terror engineered in the name of Islam, which some Muslim intellectuals, such as Sadiq al-Mahdi and the Republican Brotherhood leader, Mahmud Muhammad Taha, could not countenance. Ultimately, Taha was hanged for his opposition to the Islamization, and within 18 months of Sudan's "Islamic Experiment,"[27] popular opposition to it and to Numayri reached the point of massive demonstrations, leading to the overthrow of the regime.

During the one-year transitional government headed by Jazuli Dafa'allah, the September Laws and their apparatus for application were frozen. The job of removal or reform of the sharia was left to a coalition government elected in 1986 and led by Umma Party head, Sadiq al-Mahdi. Although Sadiq had been jailed by Numayri for his opposition to the September Laws, as prime minister he was less decisive. His public position was for moderation and compromise. He considered that Islamization under Numayri was improperly imposed and, in practice, un-Islamic, but abrogation of the sharia was not a political option that he entertained. On this point the pressure exerted on Sadiq al-Mahdi by the National Islamic Front (NIF), headed by his brother-in-law, Hasan al-Turabi, was keenly felt. In some respects his middle of the road position was a replay of party politics at the time of independence when the Umma Party called for a greater role for Islam within the context of a parliamentary republic; at that time, however, the Islamic Right was less powerful and more isolated. Until his last days in office, Sadiq was promising to introduce new Islamic laws or revise or reform them in such a way as to protect Sudan's non-Muslim minority. Impatient with these seemingly empty promises and with his failure to initiate talks with the SPLM/SPLA, Sadiq's coalition partner and the constituent assembly called for the resignation of the government. A move to circumvent Sadiq's position and abrogate the September Laws in June 1989 may have been what precipitated the 30 June coup, which is now widely recognized to have had the support of the NIF. This view has been confirmed by one insider, the former speaker of the constituent assembly, Mohamed Ibrahim Khalil.[28]

The NIF, a direct outgrowth of the Muslim Brotherhood whose image was somewhat tarnished by its close association with the Numayri regime in its last years, was organized in 1985 just after the demonstrations and the coup. Its charter, drafted in 1987, recognizes that Muslims are the majority in Sudan and, therefore, that Islamic jurisprudence should be the general source of law for the nation because it represents the will of the democratic majority (II.B). Further, the Sudanese nation is a diverse yet unified whole, and regional self-rule is best accomplished through a federal system of power sharing (III.A).[29] Although the NIF accepts the central principles of national unity and regional government, in practice it did not enter into any consensus agreement with the other major parties regarding peace talks with the SPLM before the June 1989 coup, nor has it succeeded since in fulfilling its promise to begin the peace process. Indeed, editorials in the few legal government publications hint that the current regime is prepared to leave the south to the "secessionists." Even scholars sympathetic to the NIF are writing that "the desirability of maintaining this unitary state is doubtful"[30] if a unified Islamic republic does not succeed in bringing an end to the conflict.

From a southerner's viewpoint, accustomed to disappointment and disillusionment from northern politicians, this represents a new dimension of the "jellaba mentality" that has seen the south as a source for the extraction of wealth but never as a real political partner in the future of Sudan. The southerner's deep distrust and long-held fear of Arab Muslims has intensified during the past seven years of civil war with its massive dislocation of people, a war-induced famine that affects hundreds of thousands of Sudanese, and with mutual recriminations among each of the four governments in Khartoum since 1983 and the SPLM/SPLA.

Added to the breakdown of official contacts between Khartoum and the SPLM/SPLA are reports of marauding Arab militias, especially among two sections of the Baqqara armed by Sadiq's government, and who have allegedly engaged in slavery. These activities were first reported in 1987 by a University of Khartoum professor, Ushari Mahmud,[31] who was arrested by both Sadiq and Umar al-Bashir governments for his exposé. A more recent report by the human rights group, Africa Watch, concludes that there is sufficient evidence from reports of kidnapping, hostage-taking, pawn brokering, and other monetary transactions involving human beings "on a sufficiently serious scale as to represent a resurgence of slavery."[32] The Khartoum government's failure to enforce the Sudanese law against slavery has been cited as negligence or complicity, while the central government responds that these practices are part of the customary law of the Baqqara with which it has no right to interfere. Even if these allegations prove to be false, the exacerbation of fear and hatred of the "Arab" northerner by the southerner that they represent has only served to sharpen the polarization of this deeply divided nation.

Conclusions

This new level of polarization that Sudan has been experiencing is not without its ironies. In the immediate post-independence period the southern resistance, Anya-Nya, fought to separate from the north, while the current movement, SPLM/SPLA, is struggling for a unified, democratic, and secular Sudan. The Islamists, who had visions of a unified "Islamic Republic of the Sudan," are apparently concluding, with considerable frustration, that this may be impossible and that a separated south might be the only solution. For the NIF-backed current regime, there can be no compromise on the question of sharia and Islamization. Before meeting with the SPLM they are demanding a cease-fire, which the SPLM/SPLA refuses unless the sharia is withdrawn. This stalemate amounts to a showdown over the future of Sudan as a national entity. Long-term observers of Sudan are reluctantly reaching the unpleasant conclusion that the issue is no longer who will rule Sudan but whether or not Sudan will be able to survive in any meaningful fashion.[33]

The distrust between those who have come from the north to exploit or to rule and the peoples of the south has a historical time frame of at least 150 years, spanning Ottoman and British colonial control of Sudan and 34 years of independence. While the jellaba may have exploited the southern Sudanese in an internal colonial-like relationship, the northerner was formally defeated and colonized by powers such as the British, who were seen as anti-Muslim, or the Turko-Egyptians, who, in the mahdist view, betrayed Islam. In both views Islam was a powerful mobilizing force against the enemy outsider. Today the "enemies" of Islamization are Sudanese nationals—southerners and northern secularists—who present a far more complicated case. The mobilizing effect of calls to Islamic solidarity confront and confound the integrity and unity of the nation-state. Pursuit of the Islamist agenda in Sudan has been and will continue to be met with forceful resistance and, ultimately, will be found to be inconsistent with the maintenance of national unity. Excepting the NIF, in effect currently in power, this fact has been substantially recognized by all of the major political parties, including the SPLM, in joint declarations signed at Koka Dam in Ethiopia on March 24, 1986, in the National Democratic Alliance Charter of 1989, and in a recent joint statement signed in Cairo in March 1990.[34]

The Islamist agenda has been pursued farther in Sudan than in many of the better-known examples of contemporary Islamic republics with respect to Islamization of law and application of the hudud penalties. Sudan may have some unique features with respect to its large non-Muslim minority population and years of civil war, but it nonetheless shares in the regional and global phenomenon of Islamic revival. The issues that Sudanese Islamization raises—among them the protection of the rights of non-Muslim minorities and the serious problem that issue presents for the future of the nation-state—would benefit from more research and evaluation by scholars of Islam and the Middle East.

NOTES

1. John L. Esposito, "Sudan's Islamic Experiment," *The Muslim World*, vol. 76, nos. 3–4 (1986); John O. Voll, "Revivalism and Social Transformation in Islamic History," *The Muslim World*, vol. 76, nos. 3–4 (1986); Mahmoud Mohamed Taha, *The Second Message of Islam*, trans. and introduction by Abdullahi Ahmed An-Na'im (Syracuse NY: Syracuse University Press, 1987).

2. Carolyn Fluehr-Lobban, *Islamic Law and Society in the Sudan* (London: Frank Cass, 1987); and idem., "Islamization of Law in the Sudan," *Legal Studies Forum*, vol. 11, no. 2 (1987); Carey N. Gordon, "The Islamic Legal Revolution: The Case of the Sudan," *The International Lawyer*, vol. 19, no. 3 (1985).

3. David D. Chand, "The Imposition of Shari'a Law in 1983 and the Civil War in the Sudan" (Paper presented at the eighth annual conference of the Sudan Studies Association, Providence, RI, April 1989).

4. P. M. Holt and Martin W. Daly, *The History of the Sudan from the Coming of Islam to the Present Day*, 3rd ed. (Boulder, CO: Westview Press, 1989).

5. As quoted in Abbas Ibrahim Muhammad Ali, *The British, the Slave Trade and Slavery in the Sudan, 1820–1881* (Khartoum: Khartoum University Press, 1972), p. 67.

6. *Ibid.*, p. 68.

7. Yusuf Fadl Hasan, "Some Aspects of the Arab Slave Trade from the Sudan 7–19th Centuries," *Sudan Notes and Records*, vol. 58 (1977), p. 80.

8. Muhammad Ali, *British and Slavery*, p. 69.

9. Robert O. Collins, *The Southern Sudan, 1883–1898* (New Haven, CT: Yale University Press, 1962); Dunstan M. Wai, *The African-Arab Conflict in the Sudan* (New York: Africana Publishing Co., 1981).

10. Oliver Albino, *The Sudan: A Southern Viewpoint* (London: Oxford University Press for the Institute of Race Relations, 1970), p. 77.

11. Francis M. Deng, *The Man Called Deng Majok* (New Haven, CT: Yale University Press, 1986), p. 41.

12. Umar al-Naqar, *The Pilgrimage Tradition in West Africa* (Khartoum: Khartoum University Press, 1972); M. Hiskett, "The Nineteenth-Century Ji-

hads in West Africa," in *The Cambridge History of Africa*, vol. 5, from c. 1790 to c. 1870, ed. John E. Flint (London: Cambridge University Press, 1976).

13. John O. Voll, "Revivalism and Social Transformation."

14. Holt and Daly, *History of the Sudan*, p. 87.

15. *Ibid.*, p. 86.

16. Gabriel Warburg, *Islam, Nationalism and Communism in a Traditional Society: The Case of the Sudan* (London: Frank Cass, 1978). See the introduction.

17. *Ibid.*, p. 8.

18. Fluehr-Lobban, *Islamic Law in the Sudan*, p. 36.

19. Francis M. Deng and Robert O. Collins, *The British in the Sudan, 1898–1956* (Stanford, CA: Hoover Institution Press, 1984), p. 231.

20. Muddathir Abd al-Rahim, *Imperialism and Nationalism in the Sudan* (Oxford: Clarendon Press, 1969), p. 106.

21. Muddathir Abd al-Rahim, "Arabism, Africanism and Self-Identification in the Sudan," in *The Southern Sudan and the Problem of National Integration*, ed. Dunstan M. Wai (London: Frank Cass, 1973), p. 41.

22. "An Islamic Constitution," *Sudanow*, November 1979, p. 12.

23. Dunstan M. Wai, *The African-Arab Conflict*, pp. 88–89.

24. Mohamed Omer Beshir, *The Southern Sudan: From Conflict to Peace* (London: C. Hurst and Co., 1975), p. 100.

25. Gordon, "Islamic Legal Revolution"; Esposito, "Sudan's Islamic Experiment"; Fluehr-Lobban, "Islamization of Law"; Abdullahi Ahmed An-Na'im, "Constitutionalism and Islamization in the Sudan," *Africa Today*, vol. 36, nos. 3–4 (1989).

26. Carolyn Fluehr-Lobban, "Shari'a Law in the Sudan: History and Trends since Independence," *Africa Today*, vol. 28, no. 2 (1981).

27. Esposito, "Sudan's Islamic Experiment."

28. Mohamed Ibrahim Khalil, "Crisis of Democracy and National Reconciliation" (Banquet lecture at the ninth annual conference of the Sudan Studies Association, Lexington, KY, April 1990).

29. National Islamic Front, *Sudan Charter, National Unity and Diversity*, January 1987, reprinted in *Management of the Crisis in the Sudan*, Proceedings of the Bergen Forum, February 1989, eds. Abdel Ghaffar M. Ahmed and Gunnar Sorbø, University of Bergen, 1989, pp. 133–144.

30. Abdelwahab Osman El-Affendi, "Islam and Legitimacy in the Sudanese State" (Paper presented at the ninth annual conference of the Sudan Studies Association, University of Kentucky, Lexington, KY, April 1990.)

31. Ushari Ahmed Mahmud and Suleyman Ali Baldo, *Al Diein Massacre: Slavery in the Sudan* (Khartoum 1987).

32. Africa Watch, *Denying "the Honor of Living." Sudan: A Human Rights Disaster* (New York: Africa Watch, 1990).

33. John O. Voll, "Political Crisis in Sudan," *Current History*, vol. 89 (1990), p. 179.

34. The Koka Dam declaration (A Proposed Programme for National Action) was signed by all of the major political parties in the Sudan, including the SPLM and, at a later date, the Democratic Unionist Party, but not the National Islamic Front. The text of the declaration is reprinted in Ahmed and Sorbø, *Management of the Crisis in the Sudan*, pp. 130–32.

The *Sharia* in Sudan

IMPLEMENTATION AND REPERCUSSIONS

Gabriel R. Warburg

In September 1983 President Jaafar al-Numayri officially announced the implementation of the *sharia* in Sudan. The first step was rather theatrical because it involved pouring thousands of bottles of whisky and other alcoholic beverages—worth over 3 million Sudanese pounds—into the Nile. Next followed implementation of the *hudud*, which involved public amputations of hands for stealing and other punishments prescribed by the sharia. In February and March 1984, the so-called Islamic economy was implemented with the abolishment of interest on internal transactions and replacement of income and other taxes by the prescribed *zakat*. In June of that year, Numayri ordered all his officers to swear allegiance to him personally as the imam of the Sudanese *umma*. This *bay'a* was enacted 103 years after Muhammad Ahmad ibn Abdallah received the bay'a from *akbar al-mahdiyya*, the first adherents of the newly declared Sudanese mahdi. Finally, on January 18, 1985, Mahmud Muhammad Taha, the revered 76-year-old leader of the Republican Brothers, was executed on the charge of apostasy despite repeated pleas for mercy both from within the Muslim world and from the international community. On April 6, 1985, Numayri was deposed while en route from Washington to Cairo.

Although there were many reasons for his removal, the implementation of the sharia seemed to loom large in the background. Numayri's regime was brought to an end by a broad coalition of trade unions, professionals, student organizations, and political groups. In many respects it was not unlike the fall of General Ibrahim Abbud, who was deposed in October 1964 by a civilian uprising led by associations of professionals and trade unions. Both in October 1964 and in April 1985 the army refused to intervene once it realized that the use of force would lead to a blood-bath. Here, however, the similarity ended because in 1964 army officers returned to their barracks whereas after the April 1985 uprising the army remained in control of Sudanese politics for a year, with the tacit blessing of the two most popular religious sectarian movements in Sudan—the neo-mahdist Ansar and the Khatmiyya sufi order.

In the 16 years that they were in power, Numayri and his colleagues had brought Sudan full circle in a return to its sectarian starting point. When the Free Officers came to power in May 1969, there were few issues on which they were in full agreement. Their determination to destroy sectarianism was one of these, and it led to the massacre of the Ansar in March 1970 and the confiscation of all mahdist property in the months that followed. Although lands belonging to the Khatmiyya were also appropriated in July 1970, the latter were treated less harshly than their Ansari rivals. This so-called progressive radical phase came to an end following an abortive communist coup in July 1971, replaced by a period of minor reforms. Following the execution of the communist leaders, Numayri performed the *hajj* to Mecca in late 1971 and, during his stopover in Jidda, met with Muslim Brotherhood leaders who had escaped from Sudan. This first attempt at reconciliation was rejected by Numayri's advisers following his return to Khartoum. While in Saudi Arabia, Numayri had long discussions with King Faysal regarding a new Islamic phase in Sudanese politics. Although there was no immediate follow-up with respect to the return of the Muslim Brotherhood to active politics, these meetings paved the way for the new constitution of May 1973.

According to one report, Numayri had promised King Faysal that the constitution would turn Sudan into an Islamic state, although this was opposed by some of his closest advisers. Hence, the amended version that was finally approved did not satisfy the Saudis, and the bankrupt Sudan had to manage without the aid that previously had been promised by King Faysal. After September 1983, the ideological gap between the "two Numayris"—the secular leftist leader of the May 1969 revolution and the imam Numayri, implementing the sharia and demanding the bay'a from his adherents—seemed remarkable.[1]

The Islamic Path

If one examines Numayri's self-proclaimed "Islamic path"—starting with national reconciliation in 1977 and ending with the arrests of former prime minister Sadiq al-Mahdi in September 1983 and Muslim Brotherhood leader Hasan al-Turabi in March 1985—one is struck by its complete failure, even among its most natural supporters such as the Ansar. Numayri's Islamic beliefs and policies were described in three books, two of which were ascribed to his authorship. The first, *Ai-Nahj al-Islami limadha?* (Why the Islamic Path?), was published in Cairo in 1980. It described the reasons for Numayri's shift from nationalist leftist tendencies in the early years of his rule to a strict observance of Islam in the mid-1970s. The second book, also attributed to Numayri's authorship, was titled *Al-Nahj al-Islami kayfa?* (The Islamic Path How?). It was scheduled to be published in August 1983, but appeared only in April 1985, the month of Numayri's deposal. It was intended to explain and illustrate how the Islamic path was to be implemented. The third book contains the proceedings of an international Islamic conference, held in Khartoum in September 1984, to celebrate the first anniversary of the implementation of the sharia and to eulogize the "great imam," Jaafar al-Numayri. It was published by the Sudanese parliament under the title *'Am 'ala tatbiq al-sharia al-Islamiyya fi al-Sudan* (One Year since the Implementation of the Islamic Sharia in the Sudan). In *Why the Islamic Path?*, Numayri ascribed to the abortive communist coup of July 1971 the beginning of his shift to strict Islam. He glorified the nineteenth-century Mahdiyya and its founder, Muhammad Ahmad al-Mahdi.

Even more revealing was Numayri's attitude toward the Ansar, the present-day followers of mahdism, and their acting imam, Sadiq al-Mahdi. If one bears in mind that the latter had been in open opposition to Numayri's regime from the very beginning and had tried to overthrow him as late as July 1976, Numayri's praise could only be viewed as part of a major shift in policy.[2] The connection between an "Islamic revival" and a reconciliation with the one-time "sectarian enemies" of the May 1969 revolution was no coincidence. It occurred at a time when militant Islam was forging ahead in Iran and other Muslim states. No less important was the fact that under President Anwar al-Sadat, the Muslim Brotherhood and Islamic student organizations in Egypt had risen to new prominence. Furthermore, poverty-stricken Sudan was in an ever-growing need of economic aid from its oil-rich Arab neighbors—Saudi Arabia, in particular. The Islamic path and reconciliation with the Ansar and the Muslim Brotherhood could, therefore, be viewed by Numayri as politically wise and potentially profitable. Finally, secular Nasir-style nationalism and leftist ideologies, which had accompanied Numayri's regime in its initial stages, had been discredited in Sudan as elsewhere.

Numayri's "return to Islam" was ascribed by some observers to his close spiritual association, beginning in the early 1970s, with the Abu Qurun Sufi order, which regarded the fifteenth century of the *hijra* as a turning point in the history of Islam. They believed in effect in a "second coming" of a great mahdi who will be one of their adherents. Francis Deng, in his political novel, *Seed of Redemption*, described a president's encounter with God, in which he was ordered to reform his ways and to return to the true path of a believer. On the following morning "President Munir" sent for his "local spiritual leader" in order to receive his guidance:

> . . . "Mr. President", said the mystic, "by revealing Himself, it is clear that God has chosen you to be the leader of this country. You are President, but you are also the Imam of God. He will change you as he desires. I am but a tool of His will. The power to transform you has already descended from God".[3]

Numayri's association with Shaykh Abu Qurun led to subsequent cooperation with his son, Nayal Abu Qurun, and Awad al-Jid Ahmad, both of whom had graduated from the faculty of law in the 1970s.

Following Numayri's initiation into their order, he appointed the two as judicial assistants in the president's palace.[4]

Earlier, a special committee, *lajnat muraja't al-qawanin li'tatamasha ma'a al-sharia* ([for the] revision of the laws so that they are in line with the sharia), had been put under the chairmanship of the Muslim Brotherhood leader, Hasan al-Turabi. The committee was entrusted, as its title suggests, with bringing Sudan's legislation into full harmony with the sharia and began its work as early as 1977. It drafted seven bills on such matters as the prohibition of alcoholic beverages, the banning of usury (*riba*), and gambling. Other draft bills were concerned with the implementation of the hudud prescribed in the sharia for murder, theft, adultery, and the like, but most important was the draft bill on the sources of judicial decisions because it provided for the application of the sharia in all matters not covered in other legislation. Numayri, however, was in no hurry to implement these new bills. Indeed, in the first five years of the committee's work, only the bill regulating the payment of zakat was approved, probably because it was the least controversial.[5]

Following unanimous endorsement of the Islamic path by the Sudan Socialist Union's (SSU) national congress, the process of actual legislation started in earnest in July and August 1983, when Numayri appointed a new committee consisting of three lawyers loyal to him who were entrusted with the task of transforming Sudan's legal system into an Islamic one.[6] The acts drafted by this committee, based in part on the earlier drafts of Turabi's committee, were enacted into Provisional Republican Orders and confirmed, without any debate, by the People's Assembly in its November 1983 session during two brief sittings. The most significant of these was the Sources of Judicial Decisions Act, mentioned earlier, which paved the way for the implementation of the sharia. In addition, the new penal code, the Code of Criminal Procedure, the Civil Procedure Act, and the Civil Transaction Act were enacted to facilitate the "just and fast execution" of the newly implemented hudud.

The actual process by which the foundations of the Islamic state were laid was described by Numayri in his opening speech to an international Islamic conference in Khartoum on September 22, 1984. In justifying the new measures, Numayri alluded to practical reasons. The crime rate in Sudan had risen to such a level that all previous measures had proven ineffective. In the year prior to the implementation of the hudud, nearly 12,500 murders or attempted murders had been committed, while the number of thefts had risen to nearly 130,000. According to Numayri, the crime rate had dropped as a result of the new punishments by more than 40 percent in one year. The deterrent effect of the hudud had thus been proven beyond reasonable doubt, and it was more than likely that Sudan would soon be free of crime. The essence of the implementation of the sharia was, therefore, the creation of a righteous individual leading ultimately to a just society, as prescribed by Islam.

Moving to the economic sphere, Numayri proudly ascribed his "success" to the implementation of the zakat and taxation act. Thereafter, the zakat had become the heart of Sudan's economy because it was one of the pillars of Islam, enabling the poor to receive their rightful share of the national income. As for non-Muslims, a similar tax was imposed on them. In no case would taxes on individual income exceed 2.5 percent, while tax on capital gains would not exceed 10 percent. As a result of these "benevolent taxes" Sudan, according to Numayri, had been able to attract massive investments both from foreign markets as well as from local private entrepreneurs. Finally, Numayri devoted part of his speech to the southern problem, which, in his view, was the result of an imperialist plot. For him, it was not a matter of religious rivalry because the number of Muslims in the south exceeded that of Christians, and the majority of the population were neither Muslims nor Christians but adhered to their own indigenous religions. The sharia had, therefore, no implications for the south where everyone could freely practice religion without interference.[7]

In one of his last interviews, Numayri claimed that as the imam of Sudan, to whom total obedience was dictated by Islam, it was he alone who could interpret laws and decide whether they were in line with the sharia. In assuming the title of imam, uncommon in Sunni Islam, he seemed to have been tempted by the all-embracing powers of the Shi'i imam prevailing in Iran under Ayatollah Ruhollah Khomeini. This idea of leadership as embraced by Numayri can also be traced to mahdist ideology. First, one cannot escape the similarity with the manifestation of Muhammad Ahmad as mahdi in June 1881. Shaykh al-Qurashi wad al-Zayn, a spiritual leader of the Sammaniyya order to which Muhammad Ahmad belonged, not only appointed him as his successor but also told his followers that the expected mahdi would be one of his adherents, namely Muhammad Ahmad.[8] Numayri's "appointment" by Shaykh Abu Qurun was probably an attempt to follow in the mahdi's footsteps. Second, Sadiq al-Mahdi, the mahdi's great grandson, claimed that mahdism—both in its nineteenth-century origins and at present—acted as a bridge between Shia and Sunna. He thereby inadvertently legitimized Numayri's claim to an all-embracing Shi'i concept of leadership.[9]

It is hard to examine the truth regarding Numayri's claim about the decline in the number of crimes committed in Sudan in 1985 because there seems to be no independent statistical evidence that could either refute or corroborate this. In the economic field, Numayri's claims are much easier to disprove, because his policy was a disaster with far-reaching repercussions. In 1983 Sudan was beginning to recover economically as a result of massive foreign aid and careful economic planning. The "Islamic economy" interrupted and halted this process. The Civil Transactions Act of February 1984 abolished limited liability and interest charges on all transactions not involving foreign interests. Confidence in the already shaky economy was thus further undermined. Even more disastrous was the Zakat and Taxation Act of March 1984 whereby revenue from previous taxation was virtually stopped; the new act was so obscure that it could not be implemented. The only revenue collected was the flat rate of 2.5 percent on personal incomes exceeding 200 Sudanese pounds (at that time $154) per month. Zakat on agricultural production and livestock was not even implemented because of the act's obscurity. A further loss in government revenue resulted from the ban on alcoholic drinks. Although estimates fluctuated between $30-$300 million a year, the higher sum seems more in accord with previous data. The final blow to the ailing economy was dealt by the Islamization of the banking system in December 1984, which was undertaken despite repeated warnings from some of Numayri's closest advisers. The severe economic crisis that heralded the coming of the new year was thus, at least partly, brought about by the so-called Islamic economic policy.[10]

Protagonists and Antagonists

Numayri's close association with the Muslim Brotherhood began in 1977 when, following "national reconciliation," Hasan al-Turabi and his colleagues returned to active politics. As chairman of the legislative committee and, subsequently, Sudan's attorney-general, Turabi was in a position to influence government policy to an extent that exceeded the political power of the Muslim Brotherhood, whose support was limited at that time to an important but relatively small section of the urban elite. Who were the Muslim Brothers and why was their collaboration so important for Numayri when he set out on his Islamic path? Although the 1977 reconciliation had been hammered out with Sadiq al-Mahdi, Numayri's antisectarianism had not subsided over the years. The Muslim Brothers were therefore his natural allies, because their political future also depended on the end of sectarian supremacy. They had advocated a state, based on the sharia, long before the May 1969 coup and had collaborated with the Ansar in formulating an Islamic constitution for Sudan.[11]

At a conference on "Islam in the Sudan," held in Khartoum by the Association of Islamic Thinking and Culture in November 1982, Turabi insisted that the reform of Sudanese laws, in accordance with the sharia, was the most urgent task facing the country. Although the final communiqué of the conference was in general agreement with the ideas of the Muslim Brotherhood, it advocated essential social reforms that should precede the gradual implementation of the sharia. Turabi's undertaking to act within this agreement was broken less than a year later when he openly supported Numayri's implementation of the Islamic laws.[12] This collaboration was justified by Turabi's fellow Muslim Brother, Makashfi Taha al-Kabbashi, in his pamphlet, *Tatbiq al-sharia fi al-Sudan bayn al-haqiqah wa'l-'itharah* (The Implementation of the Sharia in the Sudan between Truthfulness and Falsehood). For Kabbashi and others with similar views, there was never any doubt that the implementation of the sharia implied an inferior status for all non-

Muslims. Even Sudan's armed forces would accordingly become an Islamic army fighting the enemies of Islam—including "Communists, Crusaders, Zionists, Free Masons" or their Sudanese supporters—under the banner of Islam.[13]

The Ansar—the neo-mahdists—were the largest and best-organized sect in Sudan and, on the eve of independence, numbered more than 3 million. Consequently, their total obedience to their own imam—both in religious and in political matters—presented a major obstacle to the emergence of real democracy in Sudan. Since the assassination of his uncle, the imam Al-Hadi al-Mahdi, in March 1970, Sadiq al-Mahdi had fulfilled the dual role of acting imam of the Ansar and leader of the Umma Party. He and his followers rebuilt the movement in refugee camps in Libya from where the National Front, led by the Ansar, launched its most daring revolt against Numayri in July 1976. Numayri's survival was at least in part responsible for the national reconciliation that started exactly one year later. Both he and Sadiq probably realized that they could not easily defeat each other and hence decided to join forces. Each of the two antagonists believed that he could neutralize his foe through political maneuvering, but two years later it became clear that, as far as the Ansar were concerned, reconciliation had not been achieved. When Numayri announced his Islamic path in September 1983, Sadiq did not hesitate to denounce the policy as un-Islamic. In a sermon preached at the Ansar's mosque in Omdurman he stated, " . . . To cut the hand of a thief in a society based on tyranny and discrimination is like throwing a man into the water, with his hands tied, and saying to him: beware of wetting yourself. . . . "[14]

Following Numayri's deposal, Sadiq was even more outspoken. He analyzed five major legal pronouncements of Numayri's Islamic system, proving to his listeners that all of them constituted a total corruption of Islam. He also denounced all the legal decisions reached on the basis of these so-called sharia laws as totally un-Islamic, both in their spirit and in their execution. Apart from his total rejection of the way in which hudud was applied, he singled out Numayri's Islamic economy, explaining that it did not adhere to a true understanding of Islam. Sadiq supported the creation of an Islamic state provided it was based on the perfect application of *shura* (consultation) in all political issues and on social justice in its economic policy. The implementation of the sharia—based on current *ijtihad* (independent judgment)—would take into account current conditions and derive its judgment from the Quran and the Sunna.

Islam and Southern Sudan

One of the gravest repercussions of Numayri's Islamic phase was the renewal of hostilities in the south in 1983. Until then the Addis Ababa agreement of February 27, 1972, had rightly been regarded as the most important, if not the only, achievement of the Numayri regime. It had put an end to 17 years of internecine strife and had courageously granted recognition to the pluralistic nature of Sudanese society. In awarding the south regional autonomy, the Muslim-dominated regime acknowledged that culture, race, religion, and economics dictated a new approach to the internal structure of Sudan. This was, in fact, part of a plan to decentralize Sudan, especially in the sphere of economic development, which had been aired by the Numayri regime since 1971. The size of Sudan, the immense differences between its regions, and the concentration of economic and political power in the hands of a nonrepresentative northern elite, had evoked strong criticism of the preferential treatment granted to the central northern Sudan at the expense not only of the south but also of Darfur and Kordofan in the west and the Beja tribes of the Red Sea hills in the east.[15]

The Addis Ababa agreement had provided for equality of all citizens regardless of race, color, or religion. It recognized southern cultural identity and, hence, proclaimed its right to legislate in accordance with its customs. Free elections to the Southern Regional Assembly were decreed and this assembly was empowered to elect its own president. The unalterable foundation of this concept was expressed in the Permanent Constitution of the Sudan, promulgated in May 1973. Articles 6 and 7 specified the principles of decentralization and promised that the details of this new system of government would be issued in the near future. Article 8 established regional self-government in the south on a permanent basis and could only be amended in accordance with the provisions of the Self-Government Act of 1972. Not less significant was the provision that non-Muslims would be governed by their own personal laws. The pluralism of Sudanese society, including its multi-religious composition, were elaborated in article 16, which promised equal treatment to all followers of "religions and spiritual beliefs" and ended by stating that " . . . the abuse of religions . . . for political exploitation is forbidden. . . . "[16] If one takes into account the realities prevailing in Sudan and the radicalization of Islam in surrounding countries, including Egypt, the 1973 constitution cannot be regarded as an extreme step toward religiosity.

Nevertheless, southern politicians were, by and large, opposed to the constitution because it specified that "Islamic Law and Custom shall be main sources of legislation" (article 9) and that Arabic would be the "official language" of Sudan. One of the most outspoken opponents was Bona Malwal, a one-time minister of culture and information under Numayri, who expressed his misgivings as early as 1977 following the reconciliation agreement. According to Malwal, Turabi regarded the weakening of the south as an essential step toward the implementation of the sharia. If there were justice in Sudan, claimed Malwal, Turabi should not only have lost his post as attorney general, but should also have been "charged with plotting to overthrow the legally constituted government of the state" because he openly advocated an Islamic coup. Southern leaders, however, had as little trust in the Ansar. Their experience with the Umma-Ansar governments in the 1960s had taught them that the traditional sectarian leadership was no better than its so-called modern followers. Indeed, according to Malwal, Sadiq had stated as early as 1966 that " . . . the failure of Islam in the southern Sudan would be the failure of Sudanese Muslims to the international Islamic cause. Islam has a holy mission in Africa and southern Sudan is the beginning of that mission."[17]

The period of peaceful coexistence between north and south began to falter following the discovery of oil in the south and Numayri's unconstitutional act of dissolving the Southern Regional Assembly and its government in February 1980. This was followed by the decentralization act, aiming to divide the south into three separate regions, and by the Regional Government Act of 1980, which divided Sudan, excluding the south, into five regions. [18] This act was probably also the result of unrest in Darfur and Numayri's desire to shift part of the responsibility to regional governments. In the south, however, it was interpreted as an assault on its autonomy and its newly discovered wealth, which should have been used for the benefit of its inhabitants. Although it is true that hostilities in the south preceded the implementation of Islamic laws, it is certain that these laws exacerbated the situation to such an extent that it soon deteriorated into a full-scale civil war under the leadership of Colonel John Garang and the Sudan People's Liberation Movement (SPLM).

The Repercussions: From Democracy to Military Despotism

In the wake of Numayri's deposal on April 6, 1985, the Sudanese were overwhelmed with their newly acquired freedom. Within two weeks after the uprising some 40 political parties had announced their existence and had declared their intention to play an active part on the political scene. Among them were the three pillars of the National Front: the Muslim Brotherhood, now renamed the National Islamic Front (NIF) and led by Hasan al-Turabi; the Ansar and their political arm, the Umma Party, under their acting imam, Sadiq al-Mahdi; and the Khatmiyya Sufi order led by Muhammad Uthman al-Mirghani, which was closely aligned with the Democratic Unionist Party (DUP). All of them had played a dominant role in the period between 1964 and 1969 and were in no small measure responsible for the failure of previous attempts to introduce democracy into Sudan.

Turabi, imprisoned in March by Numayri—who then charged the Muslim Brotherhood with causing all Sudan's ills—was released from prison on April 6, 1985, and was the first political leader to meet General Siwar al-Dhahab, Sudan's temporary head of state. Turabi expressed full support for the implementation of the sharia both in the past and the future. He praised the economic measures such as the law of zakat and the advance it had made toward a just society. His only criticism regarding the implementation of the sharia was that it was not all-embracing because it did not include important issues such as constitutional law, especially regarding the shura.

The NIF presented its platform on the southern Sudan question in

May 1985 at a conference attended by some 100 of the party's southern supporters. It stated that there were no objective reasons for the renewed hostilities, hence, the implementation of the sharia should not be affected by the on-going strife. As for the future, the NIF insisted that southern Muslims—who, according to the NIF, had suffered for so long—should at last be granted their "rightful share" of power in that region. Second, the authors hailed a continuation of the rapid Islamization of the south. Finally, the NIF asserted that "a general system based on the Islamic Sharia is a religious and political necessity to every Muslim." Because the sharia is closer than any other legal system to the African cultural heritage, and because it "protects the entity and the culture of the non-Muslims," it should be maintained as the law of Sudan, which through "its flexibility will guarantee the compromises required by non-Muslims."[19]

These views were upheld by Turabi and his colleagues throughout Sudan's third democratic episode when they consistently opposed any meaningful change in the Islamic laws and in their implementation. Turabi dismissed the outcry against the sharia as emanating from the West, which sought thereby to separate Sudan from its Arab and Muslim brothers. He also asserted that Garang's demand to abolish these laws had nothing to do with religion and was based on pure Marxist principles. In Turabi's view, the Islamic state in Sudan was a reality based on popular support, hence, those opposing it could only be alien forces against whom the banner of *jihad* should and would be raised. When the NIF joined a coalition government in May 1988 and formed, together with the Umma Party, a government of "National Agreement," it was clear that there would be no compromise on Islam, even if this meant the continuation of civil war.[20]

Muhammad Uthman al-Mirghani became leader of the Khatmiyya Sufi order in 1968 following the death of his father, Sayyid 'Ali al-Mirghani. The Khatmiyya had traditionally avoided active involvement in politics and had persisted in this line under Numayri. As head of the Sufi Islamic Revival Committee, founded in 1978, Mirghani had lent his support to Numayri's so-called Islamic policy, denouncing the rival Ansar and Muslim Brothers as "Westernized Muslims," but following Numayri's downfall, Mirghani denounced his implementation of the sharia as false, misleading, and unjust and defined his regime as based on the law of the jungle. He did, however, express his conviction that under the proper religious and spiritual guidance of trained ulama and *fuqaha'* (Islamic scholars and jurisprudents), this could soon be remedied. The Islamic republic that would emerge in Sudan would be based on the shura and on the true Islamic spirit of forgiveness, human kindness, and mercy. The main concern of Islam was human dignity wherein the individual's fate, his honor, and his property would be fully guarded. It was during these years that Mirghani played an ever-increasing role in politics, thereby reversing previous Khatmiyya traditions. Apart from his personal inclination, this was probably also due to a leadership crisis in the DUP.[21]

Of the three most prominent Muslim leaders, Mirghani was the most conciliatory toward the SPLM. Following continuous failures of Sadiq al-Mahdi and his emissaries, Mirghani undertook his trip to Addis Ababa in November 1988. He returned to Khartoum with an agreement for a cease-fire, which he had initialed with John Garang and which now had to be ratified by the government and the national assembly. Negotiations with the SPLM leadership were to be started in January 1989. Mirghani's major concession, one which Sadiq had previously refused to offer, was that the Islamic laws of September 1983 would not be included in the government's platform. It was this concession that, as expected, led to yet another government crisis because the NIF refused to accept it.

Despite their massive losses in the March 1970 massacre, the Ansar had emerged once again as the strongest sect in Sudan, and their political arm, the Umma Party, won the 1986 elections. Consequently, Sadiq al-Mahdi became the uncontested prime minister throughout the third democratic episode. His policy as prime minister in the years 1986–89 cannot be reconciled with the more liberal views he had expressed previously. Even close associates from within the Ansar and the Umma were critical of his performance and accused him of having become a spokesman of the Muslim Brothers. This was especially true with regard to his adamant refusal to revoke the Islamic laws that he himself had previously labeled as un-Islamic and that he realized constituted a major stumbling block in relations between north and south.

Sadiq al-Mahdi wrote an important treatise on the future of Islam in the relationship between north and south. He rejected the notion of the separation of church and state claiming that it could not be applied in a Muslim society. Sadiq agreed, however, with most southern grievances against Islamic laws, which would turn them into second-class citizens in their own country. Therefore, purely religious laws such as the prohibiting of alcoholic beverages or eating pork, should be imposed only on Muslims. Taxes should be levied on all citizens according to one nonreligious law, decreed by the state. Zakat should be imposed on Muslims only, while discriminatory taxes such as the *jizia* (a poll tax levied on non-Muslims) should be abolished. Because the majority of Sudanese were Muslims, however, Sadiq insisted that Islam be declared the state religion and the sharia the major source of legislation. He viewed the future of the south as fully Arabized and Islamized. This would happen as a result of several processes: first, the assimilation of tribes as a result of common agriculture and grazing lands; second, the impact of Muslim sufis, jurisprudents, and merchants settling in the south; third, economic projects emanating from the north and benefiting the south; fourth, the settlement of large numbers of southerners in northern cities; and finally, the southerners' recognition that the common enemies were imperialism and "white civilization," a realization that had even convinced black Americans to embrace Islam.[22]

When in March 1989, Sadiq was at last forced to compromise with the south, the real initiative had already passed into the hands of the Khatmiyya leadership. An alliance of trade unions, professional associations, and even sections within the army presented, on February 22, 1989, a memorandum to the Council of State clearly indicating that both the army and civilians were losing patience with Sadiq's political bungling. The last attempt to save democracy, under the leadership of the "National Salvation Government," brought about the only serious attempt to deal with Sudan's real problems. On June 30, 1989, a committee of senior lawyers, including former chief justices, a former minister of justice, and several senior advocates presented to the government a draft repealing law that, if accepted, would have brought about the final abrogation of the September 1983 laws and thus paved the way for peace talks with the SPLM. This was already too late; those in the army who—not unlike the NIF—opposed this conciliatory trend and demanded the uninterrupted implementation of the sharia, acted before the new policy could be approved.[23]

The Islamic laws promulgated by Numayri and advocated by the Muslim Brotherhood have thus outlived Sudan's third democratic episode. Under a military dictatorship, guided by radical Islamic principles, the prospects for change seem nonexistent. The problems alluded to by Sadiq al-Mahdi as having led to Numayri's downfall not only remained unsolved under Sadiq's leadership but were also exacerbated. Sudan on the eve of the coup by Umar al-Bashir, on June 30, 1989, was bankrupt financially, politically, and morally largely as a result of Sadiq's incompetent leadership, a condition that led to the inability to overcome its eternal sectarian and regional divisiveness.

In Francis Deng's *Seed of Redemption*, the following "prophetic" words were uttered by Dr. Terab, leader of the Muslim Brothers, in response to President Jaber Munir's decision to implement the sharia:

> . . . Mr. President, . . . as I have told you many times, the things you do now, which are almost certain to last for long if not forever, are the decisions and actions related to the promotion of Islam. . . . Whatever you do to consolidate the position of Islam is not only bound to be deeply appreciated by the people, which means enhancing your political image and power, but is going to be difficult or impossible to undo in the future, for they will fear provoking public reaction. . . . [24]

Although Dr. Terab was, of course, an "imaginary character," his alter ego, Hasan al-Turabi, helped to make the prophecy one that was self-fulfilling. When he realized that compromise with the SPLM might endanger his dream of the Islamic state, he apparently gave a tacit or explicit blessing to his military followers.

NOTES

1. This account is based on a series of articles written by Muzamil Salman Ghandur, a close associate of Numayri, titled "Qissat al-jaysh wal-sultah fi al-Sudan" (The Story of the Military and Authority in the Sudan), *al-Tadamun*, February 1-March 8, 1986; see also Gabriel Warburg, "Islam and State under Numayri," *Africa*, (Manchester), vol. 55, no. 4 (1985), pp. 400–13.

2. Jaafar al-Numaryi, *Al-Nahj al-Islami limadha?* (Cairo: Al-Maktab al-

Misri al-Hadith, 1980), pp. 218–223. Numayri's books were attributed to Awn al-Sharif, one of his closest associates during his Islamic phase, or to Muhammad Mahjub, his Egyptian adviser and speech writer. A common joke in Khartoum was that when Awn al-Sharif presented the final version of *The Islamic Path* to Numayri, the latter's sole contribution was "limadha" (why).

3. Francis Mading Deng, *Seed of Redemption: A Political Novel* (New York: Lilian Barber Press, 1986), pp. 205–7; the quote is taken from p. 207. The author clearly states that all characters in his novel are "purely imaginary." Deng was a previous minister of state for foreign affairs in Khartoum and ambassador of the Sudan to the United States, Scandinavia, and Canada.

4. Mansour Khalid, *Nimeiri and the Revolution of Dis-May* (London: Kegan Paul, 1985), p. 277. The author was a previous minister of state for foreign affairs under Numayri.

5. Abdullahi Ahmed An-Na'im, "The Islamic Law of Apostasy and its Applicability: A Case from the Sudan," *Religion*, vol. 16 (1986), pp. 197–224.

6. Turabi, who was at that time attorney general, was, therefore, not a member of this committee though he influenced its members. Nayal Abu Qurun and Awad al-Jid Ahmad, the two "judicial assistants," were instrumental in drafting these laws, despite their lack of previous experience.

7. *'Am 'ala tatbiq al-shari'a al-Islamiyya fi al-Sudan* (Ummdurman: Majlis al-Sha'b, 1984), pp. 17–32; see also Numayri, *Al-Nahj al-Islami kayfa?* (Cairo: Al-Maktab al-Misri al-Hadith, 1985). In the latter, Numayri deals at length with the problems mentioned above; see also An-Na'im, "The Islamic Law of Apostasy and its Applicability," p. 201.

8. Na'um Shuqayr, *Jughrafiyyat wa-ta'rikh al-Sudan* (The Geography and the History of the Sudan), 2nd ed., (Beirut: Dar al-Thaqafa, 1967), pp. 642–3.

9. See Ibrahim M. Zein, "Religion, Legality, and the State: 1983 Sudanese Penal Code," (Ph.D. diss., Temple University, 1989), especially pp. 73–5. For Sadiq al-Mahdi's views on this matter see his interview in *The Middle East*, February 1980, p. 40.

10. *African Economic Development*, December 21, 1984.

11. The following, unless otherwise stated, is based on Hasan al-Turabi's interview, "We Have Eliminated Secularism," *The Middle East*, (September 1979), as published in Khalid Duran, *Islam und politischer Extremismus, Einführung und Documentation* (Hamburg: Deutsches Orient-Institut, Sondernummer 11, 1985), pp. 71–3.

12. *Sudanow*, January 1983, pp. 22–3. See also Muddathir Abd al-Rahim and Al-Tayyib Zayn al-Abdin, eds., *Al-Islam fi al-Sudan* (Islam in Sudan) (Khartoum: Dar al-Asalah li'l-Sahafah wa'l-Nashr wa'l-Intaj al-Islami,1987).

13. This pamphlet is cited in Zein, "Religion, Legality and the State," pp. 85–91.

14. "Al-Khutba al-lati alqaha al-Sayyid al-Sadiq al-Mahdi, fi Ummdur-

man" (The Sermon Which Was Preached by Sayyid Sadiq al-Mahdi in Om-durman), September 17, 1983; the following is based primarily on Sadiq's mimeographed sermons and on his interview in *al-Musawwar,* April 26, 1985.

15. See Dennis A. Rondinelli, "Administrative Decentralization and Economic Development: the Sudan Experiment with Devolution," *The Journal of Modern African Studies,* vol. 19, no. 4 (1981), pp. 595–624. For details on Numayri's southern policy see Khalid, *Nimeiri,* especially pp. 41–62.

16. All quotations are from the official English text of *The Permanent Constitution of the Sudan,* published by the Sudanese government in Khartoum on May 8, 1973.

17. Bona Malwal, *Sudan: A Second Challenge to Nationhood* (New York: Thornton Books, 1985), pp. 30–7. Also see, idem., "Has the Sudan Eliminated Secularism," *Africa,* 98 (October 1979), as quoted in Duran, *Islam,* pp. 73–4; idem., *People and Power in Sudan* (London: Ithaca Press, 1981); the quote is on p. 41.

18. The Regional Government Bill 1980 sought to establish five regional governments in the Sudan, each with its own governor and ministers. Attached to the bill was a map in which, so it was claimed, the boundary between Kordofan and Bahr al-Ghazal had been moved so as to include the newly discovered oil in the north. On this, see also Khalid, *Nimeiri,* pp. 205–10.

19. All details are from the brochure, "The Islamic National Front Presents: The Southern Sudan Question, Review, Analysis, Proposals," (n.d.; n.p.).

20. This summary is based on Hasan al-Turabi's interviews in *al-Musawwar,* July 1, 1987, May 6, May 20, July 22, 1988; *Awraq Arabiyya,* vol. 7 (1988), pp. 62–76; *al-Majalla,* April 20, 1985; *al-Watan al-'Arabi,* April 26, 1985.

21. Mirghani's views as expressed in *al-Watan al-'Arabi* April 26, 1985, and in *al-Musawwar,* April 26, 1985, December 15, 1988, and March 17, 1989; among traditional Khatmi supporters there were many who viewed Mirghani's involvement in active politics with grave misgivings.

22. Al-Sadiq al-Mahdi, *Al-Islam wa-mas'alat janub al-Sudan* (Islam and the South Sudan Problem) (Ummdurman: Matba'at al-Tamaddun, 1985), pp. 16–20.

23. *October,* March 12, April 9, April 16, 1989. The author is grateful to Professor Mohamed Ibrahim Khalil, former spokesman of the Sudanese parliament and visiting fellow at the Woodrow Wilson Center in 1989–1990, for allowing me to make use of his very informative talk on this topic.

24. Deng, *Seed of Redemption,* p. 276.

A Missed Opportunity?

SUDAN'S STABILIZATION PROGRAM, 1979–1982

Bodour Abu Affan

The performance of Sudan's economy has been deteriorating since the 1970s. During the 1980s, the deterioration accelerated. Mass poverty, war, food shortages, inflationary pressures, and heavy reliance on foreign aid and food relief all resulted in a drastic decline of the living standard and welfare of the people. These problems became seemingly permanent features of the economy.

In the middle of this period of decline, there was a major effort to create a comprehensive program to respond to these deteriorating conditions. This was the three-year Stabilization and Adjustment Program, 1979/80–1981/82, which was initiated by Jaafar Muhammad al-Numayri and was approved and supported by the International Monetary Fund (IMF) and the World Bank. This program did not, however, arrest the decline, and it may represent a moment of lost opportunity in the development of the contemporary economic problems of Sudan.

Performance of Sudan's Economy in the Past Two Decades

During the 1970s and the 1980s, the growth rates of real Gross Domestic Product (GDP) and per capita income in Sudan steadily declined. Agricultural output, particularly food production, decreased substantially. Dwindling agricultural exports, together with expanding food imports, resulted in a widening trade deficit. Sudan's industrial sector, although biased toward import substitution, was nonetheless loaded with industries (such as assembly plants) dependent upon imports. An ever-growing scarcity of foreign exchange restricted needed imports and caused widespread underutilization of capacities.

The low productivity of the agricultural and industrial sectors was primarily due to the structural weaknesses of the economy. These were manifested in a degraded infrastructure, deteriorating services, limited technological options, a high concentration of exports in a few primary agricultural commodities, the limited size and scope of the manufacturing sector, low levels of domestic savings and investments, and huge deficits in the budget and the balance of payments. In addition, a vast unskilled labor force meant massive underemployment.

Infrastructure built and capital stocks obtained during the colonial and immediate post-independence era (i.e., since 1956) decayed and disintegrated because of poor—or a complete absence of—maintenance and renovation. Services, especially education, public health and sanitation, housing, and social welfare rapidly deteriorated over these decades.

Domestic savings declined substantially during the period. Public savings were particularly low and turned into deficits by the 1980s. Poor tax policies and administration, along with substantial subsidies to loss-making public and parastatal enterprises, were major factors contributing to low levels of public savings. At the same time, both private and public investments declined appreciably, the former largely because of the poor and unfavorable investment environment, the latter because of a lack of investment funds. Speculative investments in real estate, on the other hand, greatly increased.

Growing overall deficits that resulted from decreasing revenues and increasing expenditures can be attributed largely to erratic changes in the laws, regulations, and procedures governing revenues and to expanding extra-budgetary expenditures during the period. Budget deficits greatly contributed to the accelerating rate of inflation, which was 20–25 percent per annum during the 1970s and reached 80 percent per annum by the end of the 1980s. The deficits were largely financed by increased public borrowing from the Bank of Sudan (the country's central bank). An ever-widening resource gap was aggravated by substantial external debt-service obligations. Arrears built up that curtailed capital inflows from multilateral, regional, and bilateral sources. Sudan's failure to honor the obligations of its external debts—rescheduled four times during the 1980s—adversely affected its ability to borrow further. Thus, balance of payments deficits widened continually.

Factors Contributing to Economic Imbalances

Political instability has marked Sudan's political history since independence in 1956, accompanied by mismanagement and inappropriate economic planning and policies that resulted in distortions and misallocation of resources. For example, the nationalization and confiscation measures of the early 1970s set the stage for the increasingly inefficient operation of the economy. They eroded the then flourishing private sector (locally and foreign owned) and left the public sector in full control of almost all economic activities.

During the 1970s many new public investment projects for exportable products and import substitution were established. They were financed, in the main, by external borrowing. The public sector, however, had neither the knowledge nor the capacity to manage either the nationalized and confiscated enterprises or the new ones. Thus, the former were turned into loss-making parastatal corporations, while the production of many of the latter lagged or have yet to see the light of day. The outcome of these policies was a heavily subsidized public sector financed by increased money supply (which fueled inflation), as well as mounting external debt obligations and accumulating arrears.

Rapid population growth (3.1 percent per annum according to the 1983 census) and an influx of refugees (1.5 million in the early 1980s) and migrants from neighboring countries increased the domestic demand for consumer goods. This situation placed further pressure on the scarce resources and limited capacities of the economy. Consequently, given the structural rigidities of the supply side, inflation rose to unprecedented heights. In addition, the lack of coherent economic reform policies—and the limited institutional capacity to plan, implement, and manage reforms that could promote development—substantially contributed to the steady deterioration of the Sudanese economy and added to the already miserable living conditions of the masses.

Natural catastrophes and crises were other destabilizing factors. Sudan has faced spreading desertification in the northwest and was severely affected by the serious drought of the 1980s and the devastating flood of 1988. The resumption of civil war in the southern part of the country in 1983–84 has made it impossible to utilize the rich and potentially abundant resources of that part of the land. The war has drained the country of scarce resources, prevented all development efforts in the south, and constrained those in the north.

Not an oil-producing country, Sudan was hard hit by the rise of oil prices in 1973/74 and 1980/81, which were not offset by a comparable rise of world market prices for Sudan's export commodities and thus contributed to its deteriorating terms of trade. Moreover, the accumulated external debt arrears adversely affected the inflow of foreign capital to the country and consequently reduced available funds for implementing development projects. The total external debt of the Sudan reached $11.6 billion by the end of 1987, with debt service obligations equal to 13.6 percent of GDP and 115 percent of exports of goods and services.

The Stabilization Program of 1979–82

To change a dismal economic situation, reduce mass poverty, and increase the welfare of the population requires development that can become self-sustaining. To realize this objective, certain comprehensive programs of economic adjustment and reform are needed to rectify the structural imbalances of the economy and set in motion the process of recovery. For such programs to be effective, they should consist of both supply and demand management policies combined with institutional reforms to address the profound, chronic, and acute problems of Sudan's economy.

Aware of the grave economic situation and complexity of the problems, the Numayri government made some attempts at tackling them in the early 1980s. The only serious and comprehensive program undertaken, however, was the three-year Stabilization and Adjustment Program of 1979/80–1981/82.

This program consisted of both supply and demand management policies. It was, however, biased toward demand management and gave less attention to matters relating to the supply side. The main objectives of the program were: (1) to achieve a real growth rate of gross domestic product (GDP) of 4 percent per year over the period of the program; (2) to moderate the rate of inflation from 25 percent per year to 10 percent per year by the end of the program in 1981/82; (3) to reduce substantially the proportion of government operating deficits that were financed through domestic borrowing; and (4) to contain the deficits on the balance of payments current account by curtailing imports and promoting exports.

The policy measures needed to help carry out these two objectives had two aspects that in effect made them separate programs. There was a program of monetary and fiscal stabilization and a program of rationalization of development expenditures.

Monetary and Financial Aspects of the Program

The program of monetary and financial stabilization contained significant and far-reaching measures to deal with the imbalances of the balance of payments. These included exchange-rate and trade-policy measures such as the dismantling of the massive foreign-exchange control system and the abolition of the nil-value license system and barter imports.

Other aspects of the monetary and financial program involved the creation of a parallel foreign exchange market with a par value of LS. 1 = \$1.25 to finance a wide variety of imports (about 54 percent of total imports). This amounted to a 50 percent devaluation of the Sudanese pound (LS.) to discourage imports and save foreign exchange. This rate was equal to that then prevailing in the black market. There was also the declaration of an official foreign exchange market with a par value of LS. 1 = $2.00, applicable to almost all exports (about 96 percent of total exports) and to a variety of imports deemed absolutely necessary and basic for the livelihood of most of the population (such as wheat, flour, sugar, pharmaceuticals) and imports essential for production (such as fertilizers, pesticides, and petroleum products). These commodities constitute about 46 percent of total imports. This new rate amounted to a 20 percent devaluation in the Sudanese pound, designed to avoid sustained increases in the prices of essential commodities and, as a result, to diminish inflationary pressures.

There was a declaration that the remittances of Sudanese nationals working abroad were to become a part of the parallel market operations. This provided an incentive for expatriate Sudanese to send their remittances through official channels, facilitating an efficient use of foreign exchange resources and increasing the supply of scarce foreign exchange. The program also included permission for residents and non-residents of Sudan to maintain foreign-exchange current accounts in local banks for free use in import financing.

The program aimed at the reduction of bank-financed fiscal deficits from LS. 132 million in 1978/79 to LS. 100 million in 1981/82—a reduction of about 30 percent—and the reduction of government expenditures by LS. 43 million in the 1979/80 budget. By carrying out a comprehensive reform of the tax structure and administration in collaboration with the International Monetary Fund (IMF), the aim was an increase in revenues and a mobilization of resources during the second and third years of the program and beyond.

The program also addressed the problems of accumulated external debt arrears, which at that time amounted to $1.2 billion. Overdue payments on foreign-debt arrears, as well as those debts which were falling due during the program period, had been rescheduled by the end of 1979. The IMF and World Bank paved the way for Sudan to reach the first rescheduling agreement with its Paris Club creditors. In the context of this agreement, Sudan was committed to limiting new external borrowing during the program period to development and other medium- and long-term loans and grants, and to refrain from short-term borrowing at commercial rates.

There was to be an effort to increase export earnings by promoting the growth of exports. To implement this, more incentives were given to producers of the various export crops. For example, the export tax on cotton—the chief export crop—was abolished, and land and water charges on non-exportable crops (or less important cash crops in the irrigated subsector) were levied to realign the cost/price structure in the irrigated subsector. The area under cotton cultivation was also to be progressively increased during the program period so as to achieve rapid expansion in the output of this crop.

In support of this monetary and fiscal stabilization program, Sudan's government obtained balance of payments support from a variety of sources. The IMF provided SDRs 200 million (about $250 million) under its Extended Fund Facilities (EFF) over the program period. Saudi Arabia provided about $400 million over the same period. Other friendly countries contributed significant commodity aid.

Development Expenditure Program

A major aspect of the whole stabilization and adjustment program entailed a three-year development program. The priorities of this development effort were: (1) the completion of on-going projects in the shortest possible time and a halt to the initiation of new projects; (2) the rehabilitation of completed projects, particularly those in the export sector, where productivity had been declining because of the deterioration of capital stock (cotton production was given special attention and emphasis); (3) the improvement of the existing infrastructure, particularly in the transport and energy sectors, to ease bottlenecks in production and distribution.

For the rehabilitation of the export sector, the World Bank approved substantial International Development Association (IDA) credits under Agricultural Rehabilitation Programmes I and II (ARP I and ARP II) in 1980 and 1982 respectively. These credits were allocated for rehabilitating the irrigated agriculture sub-sector that mainly produces cotton.

Adequate financial support for the implementation of this whole program was to come from the proposed expansion of revenues and contraction of government expenditures under the stabilization program, combined with the foreign assistance that was forthcoming in the form of balance-of-payments support and rehabilitation credits. Also, the World Bank, the African Development Bank, many regional financial institutions, and bilateral donors advanced rehabilitation credits for Sudan. This assistance provided additional funds for the implementation of all of the measures set out in the program.

During most of the period of the program, further policy measures were undertaken. Most pronounced were the succesive devaluations of the Sudanese pound and the application of the new exchange rates (after devaluation) to about 94 percent of imports and all exports except the major ones of cotton and gum arabic. For cotton and gum arabic the adjustment was partial. Subsidies on certain commodities were decreased, and the prices for sugar and petroleum were subjected to an upward revision in 1981/82.

Evaluation of the Program

By the end of the program period the verdict was that it had been a failure. Although it consisted of a comprehensive package that encompassed both demand and supply policies, action on the exchange rate was the only element of the total package that was emphasized. The various other plans for reform were not implemented in a consistent and coherent manner. The program was applied unevenly and was characterized by ad hoc policies implemented at times of crisis with little or no consistency of approach.

An analysis of the statistics provided in the table of key economic indicators (Table 1) reveals that, despite all the efforts of the program, little progress was achieved in reducing the structural imbalances of Sudan's economy, internally or externally.

GDP in real terms consistently declined over the program period and

TABLE 1
Economic Performance of Sudanese Economy (Key Economic Indicators) 1981/82–1987/88

	81/82	82/83	83/84	84/85	85/86	86/87	87/88
GDP growth rate (% p.a. at factor cost in constant prices)	3.0*	− 0.4	− 2.9	− 13.5	10.6	3.4	− 2.6
Real per capita income growth rate (% p.a.)	0.1*	− 3.5	− 6.0	− 16.6	7.5	0.1	− 5.7
Other indicators (in % of GDP)							
Domestic savings	15	8	8	5	5	1	
Public	2	− 7	− 3	− 5	− 12	− 11	
Private	13	15	11	10	17	12	
Gross investment	19.0	17.4	16.5	16.2	12.8	10.3	
Public	5.5	4.9	4.2	3.5	1.8	3.1	
Private	13.5	12.5	12.3	12.7	11.0	7.2	
Total revenues	14.7	13.3	13.1	12.9	10.0	8.4	6.8
Total expenditures	27.9	25.2	21.5	22.0	25.8	21.1	
Overall budget deficit	− 13.2	− 11.9	− 8.4	− 9.1	− 15.8	− 12.7	
Exports (G + NFS)	9.4	8.8	10.8	10.1	7.6	6.7	
Imports (G + NFS)	25.4	25.3	23.7	24.7	18.8	17.1	
Resource gap	− 16.0	− 16.5	− 12.9	− 14.6	− 11.2	− 10.4	
Debt service obligations (including arrears)	7.5	16.1	10.4	12.4	10.3	13.6	

* Average over previous six years.

Table compiled by the author from data published in the following: Bank of Sudan, *Annual Reports* (1981–89); Ministry of Finance and Economic Planning, *Annual Economic Surveys* (1981–89); Ministry of Finance and Economic Planning, *The Four Year Salvation, Recovery and Development Programmes: 1988/1989–1991/92* (Vol. 1) (Khartoum, 1988); and idem, *A Programme of Action of the Government of Sudan, Relating to Its Economic and Financial Policies* (Khartoum, 1987).

beyond. Only in 1985/86 did it show a positive growth rate, but that was largely due to favorable weather conditions. GDP in subsequent years continued to decline and to register a negative growth rate.

Domestic savings also showed a declining trend during the period and afterwards. Government savings were negative all through, and gross investment steadily decreased. The decline of private investment was due to the unfavorable investment climate, scarcity of foreign exchange, and, thus, shortages of essential inputs and spare parts. The decline of public investment can be attributed to the diminution of foreign capital for new development projects.

The government failed to implement the necessary demand-management policies to reduce budget deficits. The tax system, which is characterized by a narrow base, limited buoyancies (less than 1.0) and widespread evasion compounded detrimental institutional and policy changes in 1983 and 1984, resulting in a considerable reduction of tax revenues. At the same time, extra-budgetary expenditures increased substantially, amounting to about one-third of total budgeted expenditures over the years 1983/84–1987/88. As a consequence, large budget deficits kept increasing every year, while the money supply increased at a high rate, partly to finance the deficit in the Central Government Budget and partly to finance the operating cost of loss-making parastatals.

Government policy to deal with the attendant inflationary pressures took the form of more administrative and price controls in an attempt to stop the rise in the cost of living. The end result of this policy, however, was to reduce profit margins and incentives for production, to create scarcities in the official economy, and a corresponding surge of the underground economy. Scarce commodities became available at black-market prices with scarcity rents thus created accruing to operators in the underground economy. More seriously, this policy diverted economic activities away from productive uses, led to a decline in investment, and prompted capital flight. Accordingly, administrative and price controls failed to reduce aggregate demand and succeeded only in increasing scarcities, expanding the underground economy, and compounding illegal profit margins. Obviously, this would be detrimental to the budget as the growth of the underground economy further eroded an already narrow tax base. The budgetary situation deteriorated further because of mounting subsidies for essential consumer goods in an attempt to alleviate the increasing inflation and maintain the elusive low-cost-of-living policy.

Exports registered a declining trend while imports did not decrease appreciably. Thus, the resource gap widened during and immediately after the program. It dropped temporarily and slightly, then stagnated at a high level. The implication of this is that the successive devaluations of the Sudanese pound carried out during the program period were ineffective. Producers of exports, who were supposed to respond positively to the increase in prices for their crops and to produce more, did not react accordingly. This was because of the rigidities of the supply side resulting from the structural constraints that characterized the economy. These impediments were not removed before, or concurrently with, the introduction of price incentives. Farmers, therefore, could not reap the benefits from devaluations. Although almost all rehabilitative efforts were concentrated on the cotton subsector, the full devaluation rates were not applied to the cotton crop. Therefore, cotton producers who might have responded positively to the increase in price for their crop—because many restraints to their production had been removed—were not sufficiently induced to do so.

Moreover, the series of devaluations of the Sudanese pound during the program period did not curb imports; because almost all imports were essential with no substitutes available, this area was relatively inelastic. They were comprised of basic foodstuffs, industrial goods, and other necessities. The outcome was more inflationary pressure (cost push) and a widening resource gap or, at best, a stagnant one at very high levels. If the program had given due attention to the food and local raw material sectors and begun to rehabilitate them, the import bill could have been reduced and the adverse impact of devaluation could have been contained by the presence of substitutes. Moreover, the need for subsidizing food imports would have vanished and budget deficits thereby reduced.

An across-the-board squeeze on government expenditures entailed a significant reduction of expenditures on social services such as education, primary health care, sanitation, water supply, and social welfare activities. Such a squeeze deprived the population of the essential human needs for a decent life.

In sum, the overall assessment of the policy measures and instruments of the Stabilization and Adjustment Programme 1979/80–1981/82 in light of the economic performance criteria of GDP is that they were ineffective in bringing about internal and external balances, let alone in alleviating poverty and attaining transformation and self-sustainable development.

The Post-Program Period

After the program period, economic conditions deteriorated very rapidly and culminated in the overthrow of the military regime of General Numayri in April 1985. A caretaker government assumed office the following year. Because of its limited term of office, this government could not introduce economic reforms, and the economy continued to deteriorate.

In May 1986, a democratically elected government came to power. From the outset, it accorded high priority to addressing the complex problems of the economy and embarked on the preparation of a Four-Year Salvation, Recovery and Development Programme 1988/89–1991/92. In view of the urgency of the situation and the fact that the Four-Year Salvation, Recovery and Development Programme would not be finalized before 1988, the government—with the help of the World Bank and the IMF—worked out a "Program of Action" in 1987/88 to stop the progressive deterioration of the economy. This program was formulated within a broad medium-term framework, aimed at achieving a sustained rate of economic growth, reducing the rate of inflation and balance of payments deficit. It embodied all the principal policy instruments of the usual adjustment programs, such as tight credit and price decontrols, privatization policies, and across-the-board reductions in budget deficits.

The Programme of Action of the civilian regime was approved and supported by the World Bank and the IMF, as well as other international donors at the Consultative Group meeting in Paris at the time.

However, the program was never actively implemented. The civilian government was unwilling to go ahead with some of the measures that entailed austerity and sacrifices, such as major exchange-rate adjustments and, most notably, the removal of subsidies on essential consumer goods. The government was also reluctant to carry out other measures that involved the laying off of workers and civil servants, especially in reforming the parastatals and the civil service. These measures were socially unacceptable and were therefore politically difficult to undertake, given the extremely fragile position of the government as a shifting and unstable coalition.

Economic conditions continued to deteriorate. The civilian government was unable to deal with the chaotic economic situation in the country. A military coup took place at the end of June 1989, and a new National Salvation Revolutionary Government was formed.

The new government pledged from the start to adopt policies designed to improve the economic situation, alleviate mass poverty, and put the economy back on the path of development and growth. It formulated and published the "National Economic Salvation Programme, 1990–1993" based on the recommendations of the National Economic Salvation Conference held in Khartoum in October/November 1989. This program emphasized the medium-term objectives of liberalization and privatization of the economy and drafted policy measures to implement these objectives. In addition, it outlined short-term measures to deal with internal and external imbalances.

The deterioration of the Sudanese economy during the 1970s and 1980s emphasizes the problems of trying to create the conditions for economic stabilization and self-sustained development. The stabilization program undertaken in the middle of this two-decade period was an effort to attack the economic problems in a relatively comprehensive and systematic way. The program followed the pattern of the usual programs recommended by governments and international agencies. However, because of the difficulties of application, it did not resolve the problems.

The stabilization program of 1979–82 provides insights into problems of resolving economic difficulties in a country like Sudan. On the basis of this experience, it may be that adjustments without transformation will not lead to a self-sustained development of Sudan's economy. Instead, it may be more effective to deviate from the standard adjustment programs and the orthodox instruments used in the past to achieve the transformation of the economy into self-sustained development.

SOURCES

Abu Affan, B. O.

"The New Economic Policies and Structural Imbalances of the Sudan Economy," *Sudan Journal of Development Research*, ESRC. Vol. 2, December 1979.

"The Public Industrial Sector: Development and Prospects," *Sudan Journal of Development Research*, ESRC. Vols. 1–2, 1981–82.

·*Industrial Policies and Industrialization in the Sudan* (Graduate College, University of Khartoum). England: Ithace Press, 1986.

"The Problems of Public Transport in Metropolitan Khartoum," *Journal of Administrative Science* (Sudan Academy for Administrative Science), June 1987.

"Social Dimension of Adjustment Programmes: Khartoum Province Study Case" (Research Report No. 20), ESRC. Khartoum, 1988.

"Suggested External Debt Strategies for a Sub-Saharan African Country: A Case Study of the Sudan," in *Proceedings of the Seminar on External Debt Problems of African and Arab Countries* (held in Libya, March 1989).

Atabani, F. A.

"Study of Exchange Rate Management and Coordination: A Case Study of Sudan," in *Proceedings of Seminar on Exchange Rate Management and Coordination in the Arab World* (held by the Arab Monetary Fund in Abu Dhabi, U. A. E., April 25–27, 1987).

Ministry of Finance and Economic Planning

A Programme of Action of the Government of Sudan Relating to Its Economic and Financial Policies (Delegation heads meeting for Sudan, held in Paris, December 1987).

The Four-Year Salvation, Recovery and Development Programme 1988/89–1991/92, Vol. 1. Khartoum, July 1988.

United Nations Economic Commission for Africa

The Khartoum Declaration on the Human Dimension to Africa's Economic Recovery and Development. Khartoum, March 1988.

African Alternative Framework to Structural Adjustment Programmes for Socio-Economic Recovery and Transformation (AAF-SAP). Addis Ababa, 1989.

Refugees and Development

DISSONANCE IN SUDAN

Mary C. Kilgour

In 1984, the Second International Conference on Assistance to Refugees in Africa (ICARA II) made a plea for development assistance in addition to relief aid for African refugees. The conference concluded that refugees in Africa, unlike those in Europe, remained in their countries of first asylum for long periods rather than seeking resettlement in third countries; they also tended to go to developing countries where their presence constituted a heavy burden on these states and the international community unless they were able to contribute to their own livelihoods and the local economy. Alleviation of this burden was not likely to happen without investment in development projects.

In response, ICARA II donor participants pledged assistance toward refugee development projects proposed by African countries, but these good intentions did not materialize to the degree hoped. The 1984–85 famine in the Horn of Africa required the immediate diversion of pledged resources to increased relief needs.[1] Since ICARA II, funding has continued to be scarce for refugee development projects. Frequent famines in East Africa (1984–85, 1987–88, and 1990) no doubt have had an effect, but they provide only a partial explanation.

Another explanation for the failure to implement ICARA II is the dissonance between problems and the policies and structures of institutions established to deal with them. This dissonance comes from the unequal pace of change and the institutional ability to respond to change. It is, it seems, the natural state of affairs. The more complex the context, the more likely there is to be grossly unbalanced change and resulting dissonance. Successful institutions are those that adapt quickly and appropriately to change, but the potential for dissonance in international settings is enormous. These are commonsensical notions, but they are the basis of social science theories of the dissemination of innovations and even of the relationship between the US Congress and the executive branch of government, to name just two examples.

This article contends that the notion of dissonance is useful in understanding the dilemma of long-term Third World refugees. Sudan is not unique in suffering from this problem, but it bears a heavy burden of it and, therefore, may be a valuable case to review. The country is facing hard times; economic decline, political instability, drought, and civil war all plague the beleaguered people, their government, and some 763,400 refugees who have sought shelter there.[2] The situation demands responses that donors cannot provide through their current policies and resource constraints. It demands development and that requires peace—something Sudan's government cannot or will not produce. All donors to Sudan contribute to the dissonance, but the United States is the major bilateral donor and, consequently, will be the main focus of this discussion along with the government of Sudan and key international agencies.

Refugees and Displaced Persons: The Magnitude of the Problem

The consequences of war have been profound for large numbers of Sudanese and their neighbors. Military actions have caused thousands of people to flee the country and seek refuge in Ethiopia, Uganda, and Zaire or to be displaced within Sudan. Adding to the problem, civil wars in neighboring countries have led to thousands of people from Ethiopia, Uganda, and Chad taking refuge in Sudan. As of early 1990, there were 663,200 Ethiopian refugees in Sudan. The vast majority settled in the eastern region of the country along the border with Ethiopia and in Khartoum and Port Sudan. They live in camps or among local communities, and about half receive international assistance from the United Nations High Commissioner for Refugees (UNHCR). Zairians in Sudan number 5,000, Ugandans 25,200, and Chadians 70,000.

Although Sudan is host to some 763,400 refugees, 426,100 of its own citizens have fled into neighboring countries.[3] The vast bulk of these people left to escape the fighting in the south and as refugees entered Ethiopia where they live in camps along the border. They receive help through the UNHCR and the World Food Program (WFP), but continue to live under extreme adversity, both physical and social.

The internally displaced Sudanese—mostly southerners who fled to northern cities or to garrison towns in the south—are in no better shape than the refugees. In the south they find themselves caught between combatants in the civil war. Reaching them with food and other needs depends on military and political access afforded by the warring factions. In 1988, 250,000 people died of war-related famine and disease, but in 1989, Operation Lifeline-Sudan managed to prevent a repeat of this. The expectation is that 1990 will fall somewhere in between.

Traditionally, Sudan has been hospitable to strangers, and its people have shown this same hospitality to the refugees in their midst.[4] In recent years, as its refugee population has increased and persisted and, as its own fortunes have declined, hospitality has worn thin. As difficult as it must have been, the government in 1987 had to tell donors it could accept no more refugees.[5] It announced that it could not recognize as refugees those fleeing climatic catastrophe, the reason why large numbers of Ethiopians had come into Sudan. The government asked for more help from the international community, however, at the very time that donors were reducing their resource transfers to Sudan.

Sudan has tried to accommodate refugees in agricultural settlement schemes either as subsistence farmers or wage earners. From the beginning, its refugee policy emphasized rural, income-generating activity. It recognized early on, well before ICARA II, that refugees would have to become self-supporting[6] and that development was essential. Many of the rural settlement schemes were developed with international assistance. The World Bank currently has one project in Sudan involving refugees whose goal is to increase agricultural production.

The project, carried out in conjunction with the UNHCR, has suffered shortcomings in implementation and has fallen behind schedule. Although this particular project is grant-financed, others that have indirectly benefited refugees have been loan-funded. These delays cost Sudan money and may even challenge the feasibility of the projects. Japan and the European Economic Community have also carried out projects as have several nongovernmental organizations (NGOs), but these responses have been inadequate to the need.

Some 1.8 million displaced Sudanese are unwelcomed squatters in greater Khartoum.[7] The government would prefer to move them outside the city and has already started that process. Unfortunately, the farther away from the city, the less employment and fewer services the displaced are likely to find. As a result they will tend to drift back into the city unless the government can find the resources to establish rural settlements for them similar to those proffered to refugees. Establishing rural settlements appears to be government policy, but is unlikely to happen under current circumstances. The large numbers of displaced who remain in Khartoum are ignored by government investment programs while some receive a modest amount of relief aid mainly from NGOs.

Economic Performance and Donor Response

Sudan's real per capita gross domestic product has declined by 27 percent since 1970.[8] There are many other indicators of a weak economy. The annual growth rate of agriculture between 1981 and 1986 was minus 3 percent[9]; international reserves declined by 45 percent between 1970 and 1987[10]; total long-term debt service as a percentage of exports increased from 9.1 percent in 1970 to 33.8 percent in 1987.[11]

Since the imposition of Islamic law in 1983, the war between the Sudan People's Liberation Army (SPLA), representing Christian and animist southerners, and the northern Muslim-dominated government has worsened and increased the drain of material and human resources that would ordinarily be used for national development. Accurate figures on the government's defense budget are unobtainable, but there is no doubt that, together with reduced revenues from a stalled economy, defense expenditures have contributed to the decline in basic services to the civilian population and in development investment generally. Figures available for the years 1975–76 to 1986–87 clearly substantiate declines in government spending for basic services and development.[12]

The war has contributed to the instability of the national government, including the overthrow of the democratically-elected government of Sadiq al-Mahdi in June 1989. This, in turn, led to the mandatory imposition by the US government of Section 513 of the Foreign Assistance Appropriations Act which immediately prohibits further economic assistance to a country whose democratically-elected government is overthrown by a military action.[13] Although it is legally possible to waive the provision, the State Department apparently does not believe there are adequate grounds to propose a waiver in the case of Sudan.

As its economic growth has slowed, Sudan has found it increasingly difficult to service its debt. Arrears to the International Monetary Fund (IMF) have grown so large that it is close to being declared a "non-cooperator," a new term reserved for the few countries, such as Sudan and Liberia, whose debt arrears have become impossibly large—a status just short of expulsion and a measure the fund seems unwilling to take. The IMF's evolving categories of membership participation to accommodate the modern world of Third World debtor nations may be constructive in that it keeps the institution talking to the debtors and maintains the Fund's own credit worthiness, but it hardly deals with the real problems of Third World debt.

Whenever a country falls more than one year in arrears on its foreign assistance loan repayments, the US government must impose the Brooke-Alexander amendment requiring that all new economic and military assistance be stopped.[14] Further, after eight months of continuous failure to pay, the assistance program must be phased out; no new funds can be obligated except for that purpose.[15] Sudan has been under the Brooke-Alexander sanctions since January 1989 so the in-country mission of the US Agency for International Development (AID) expects to terminate most of its development activity in 1990. Emergency and refugee assistance, food aid, and a few regional projects will continue.[16] Thus, the Development Assistance and Economic Support Fund budget of AID in Sudan—more than $200 million in 1984–85 when ICARA II was held—will be zero in 1991.

The laws imposing these restrictions on assistance to Sudan were aimed at countries taking actions that were seen by the US Congress as inimical to development and to the sanctity of international agreements. When the Brooke-Alexander amendment was enacted in 1976, the tremendous debt burden facing most developing countries, and the consequences in terms of economic deterioration, had not developed. Brooke-Alexander evolved during the period of recycling petrodollars which played a large part in causing the current crisis. As of December 31, 1989, some 14 countries were sanctioned under Brooke-Alexander and 5 more were approaching it.[17]

Although no one is talking yet about repealing the Brooke-Alexander amendment, there is recognition within the US government of the disruption caused by stopping and starting aid flows as developing countries struggle to keep pace with debt payments. Sudan has been in and out of "Brooke status" several times since 1985. There is also growing realization that debt relief is needed. The United States already has a forgiveness provision it can apply to traditional development assistance funds in sub-Saharan African countries,[18] but it is tied to economic policy reform and concurrence with IMF program prescriptions, and Sudan is far from qualifying. The government has tried to control the economy too tightly, and its influence on economic decision-making is expanding rather than lessening. Thus, Sudan's performance is incompatible with the prevailing view of most donor nations that economies should be privatized and released from public sector interference and that debt forgiveness must be earned. In addition, no one is talking about repealing Section 513, the provision that denies aid to regimes that overthrow democratically elected governments. Consequently, Sudan is likely to remain beyond the reach of US economic assistance resources at the time when its economy and its residents, both citizens and refugees, so badly need them. The obverse of this is that any leverage to encourage reforms in Sudan that might come from an economic assistance program is lost.

The United States is not the only donor shying away from Sudan.

The World Bank continues a modest program of about $30 million in new lending each year, but this is considerably smaller than it was a few years ago. The main reason for the reduction in the bank's program was to show solidarity with the IMF's position that Sudan's debt arrears are egregious and its economic policies unwise; other bilateral donors have responded similarly. Sudan's actions have clashed with these institutions' internal rules and policies for an effective aid relationship. The rules governing current donor-recipient relationships with respect to repayment of debt, self-help policies, and internal governance, as incongruous or counterproductive as they might be, do not support the performance of the government of Sudan. Although the rule of sovereignty allows the government to exercise absolute authority within its borders, the donor institutions can—and sometimes must, according to their own laws—resist cooperating. In short, Sudan bears the consequences of its actions, and those consequences are a reduction in foreign assistance. This reduction, in turn, contributes to the further decline in Sudan's economy and political stability. The likelihood of success for the goals of ICARA II are exceedingly low under these circumstances.

Institutional Capacities to Deal with Refugees

The large number of refugees in Sudan is not a short-term problem.[19] Yet, donors working on refugee problems are not well equipped to handle long-term problems. They have tried to cope with the changing needs of refugees, but problems have mounted faster than solutions.

Even the definition of a refugee is under challenge. The traditional definition was codified in 1951 by international agreement, expanded in 1967 by means of the international Protocol Relating to the Status of Refugees and adapted for Africa in 1969. The 1969 document describes the circumstances that confer legal refugee status,[20] but does not incorporate as refugees the famine victims who cross international borders. Consequently, the government of Sudan was on solid legal ground when it refused to recognize this category of individual. The UNHCR, however, considers them "persons of concern" and provides assistance to them, greatly expanding the UNHCR's area of responsibility.

Even though basic international conventions governing refugees date to almost 40 years ago, donors have responded worldwide in a fairly ad hoc way to ever larger numbers of refugees and to the changing nature of refugee populations. The budget of the UNHCR has grown from about $458 million in 1985 to $574 million in 1989, yet the agency is constantly strapped for funds and currently faces a major funding crisis. This may in part be attributed to management difficulties within the UNHCR, but much can be explained by the 50 percent increase in refugees and persons of concern worldwide between 1985 and 1989. In 1985, the UNHCR spent $46 per refugee per year. By 1989, this figure had dropped to $38 per capita. Considering inflation, the impact is even more severe.[21]

The UNHCR has tried to deal with the development needs of refugees. W. R. Smyser, a former deputy high commissioner, has pointed out the short planning and budgeting horizon of the UNHCR as compared with the United Nations Development Program (UNDP) with which it has collaborated on development projects for refugees, and the fact that institutions dealing with refugee programs and with development respectively, are separate.[22] John Rogge has pointed to a similar functional separation of agencies and lack of coordination within the government of Sudan.[23]

Within the US government, responsibility for refugees and development programs is divided between the State Department and AID. This division was made years ago, perhaps when refugees presented greater political than developmental challenges in their country of first asylum. The State Department Bureau for Refugee Programs has responsibility for refugees and makes grants to international agencies and nongovernmental organizations to provide assistance to them. State has no in-house development capacity, however, and is legally precluded from providing development assistance. AID has the development mandate and capacity, and a larger budget than the refugee bureau, but AID interprets its mandate to exclude assistance to refugees except with food and emergency programs. As is true with other donors, when acting bilaterally, the United States cannot easily work with citizens of one country when they reside in another country. Understandably, a poor country finds it difficult to allow development assistance to flow to foreigners when its own citizens are in need. This is obviously the case when loans are being used to finance development projects but applies to grants as well. There is only one significant example on record of refugees being major beneficiaries of a regular AID development project in Sudan—a water supply project in Port Sudan undertaken in conjunction with the UNHCR and the Cooperative for American Relief Everywhere.[24]

Emergency programs implemented by AID's Office of Foreign Disaster Assistance by definition are short term and not well suited to the sustained effort required for development activities. AID's food aid program can be used for development activities, such as food for work and policy reform support, as well as emergency situations, but the beneficiaries are citizens of the host country. When refugees are targeted, the programs are designed and carried out by the World Food Program or other international organizations using food commitments from bilateral donors.

The WFP has taken an important step in recognizing that refugees need longer-term solutions. In 1989 it recommended creating a category of pledge and internal programming called "protracted refugees" in recognition that its annual budgeting for emergencies was inappropriate for longer-term refugee problems. Now any refugee situation that persists longer than one year must receive a different form of project analysis and be presented to the Committee on Food Aid for approval as a regular program. The expectation is that more appropriate project design and better planning and, therefore, better project execution will result.[25]

Conclusions

A variety of factors constrain effective refugee assistance. The sheer number of refugees has put great strains on donor budgets held back by declining economic fortunes representing dissonance between need and response. In Sudan, conflicting policies of the government and do-

nors have led to the withdrawal of aid resources also creating dissonance. Refugees' needs are changing the longer they stay in the Sudan
and the sicker the country's economy becomes. In such cases, self-
support becomes more necessary at the very time the environment becomes less receptive. The resulting tension constitutes dissonance.

The gains made by the refugees to date are at risk, yet the situation
in the home country of most of them—Ethiopia—is deteriorating.
Fleeing the situation in Sudan is not the answer, but there are measures
that can be taken to begin to address the needs. Failing the opportunity
to return home, refugees need acceptance in Sudan and a chance to
earn a living. As Rogge has pointed out, the Sudanese people's traditional hospitality to refugees has been severely taxed, especially in the
case of urban refugees.[26] It worsens as refugees are perceived as taking
away resources needed by Sudanese citizens.[27] The challenge to the
Sudanese and to the donor community is to facilitate the refugees'
ability to earn their own living so they will be less of a financial drain
in the future. This requires investment either directly in refugees as
individuals or as a distinct group of people, or it requires investment
in economic growth in areas where refugees can benefit. The nonre-
fugee Sudanese also need to earn a living, as do the internally displaced,
and the Sudanese government's support is far more likely if the investment benefits Sudanese as well as refugees. Obviously, the problems
of refugees in Sudan are inextricably linked to Sudan's internal problems.

There has been recognition, at least since the first ICARA conference
in 1981, that more attention needs to be given to the long-term development needs of refugees, but the response has been slow. Institutions
tend to cling to what is familiar, to what they do well. Development is
not easy even under ideal circumstances, and refugee populations and
the governments that host them do not present ideal circumstances.
Sudan poses formidable challenges to the donor community and to its
own government. Persisting with the status quo of relations between
the government and donors is leading only to further decline in Sudan.
Some breakthrough is needed.

The first move unquestionably must be Sudan's. The government
cannot expect the donor community to respond to the needs of Su-

danese citizens or refugees unless the government itself demonstrates commitment. This lack of commitment is at the root of reduced donor involvement in Sudan and has led to the imposition by the US government of the punitive legislative provisions mentioned earlier. This lack of commitment to the well-being of its own citizens shows that the government is disconnected from the governed. Its two most important moves would be a concerted economic policy reform program that frees up the economy and makes some progress in seeking a solution to the civil war. Easier steps would be to be more responsive to the legitimate efforts of NGOs and donors in carrying out humanitarian and development activities. Currently, the impression commonly held is that foreigners have to plead with the government to carry out effective projects, whether developmental or emergency in nature. Travel permits, the exchange rate applicable to relief activities, NGO registration, and other bureaucratic procedures are just a few examples that have recently caused frustration among foreigners working on development and relief activities in Sudan. Many of these irritants have a negative effect on the use of resources that could bring benefits to the country.

With the right overtures from the Sudanese government, donors might respond by breaking the bonds that tie them to earlier, simpler times. The donors need to look at whether their current policies and regulations have not become counterproductive. For instance, under the right circumstances could not the United States waive restrictive legislative provisions? Although it might not be possible or desirable to make a general waiver, one specifically to provide development aid to refugees or the internally displaced might be justified on humanitarian grounds. Currently, there is a fairly sharp definition of what constitutes emergency assistance, which can be provided even when sanctions are applied, but one cannot achieve development, which is a long-term proposition, with short-term emergency assistance. Could there be some relaxation of these definitions?

For the United States to channel development assistance to refugees would also require a closer relationship between the State Department refugee bureau and AID. Apparently an experience with a transfer of funds between the agencies did not produce a satisfactory result for the bureau. A different approach could be tried with AID implementing

development programs for refugees under what is called a Participating
Agency Service Agreement (PASA), using the refugee bureau's budget
and monitoring. This would reassure Sudan that the funds were additional to those they received for their own citizens. AID has years of
experience using PASAs with other government agencies, although the
refugee bureau may be less familiar with this device. For the bureau to
increase its ability to respond to refugees' development needs, however,
its budget must increase. Although development assistance is not a
popular program in Congress, the argument has not yet been made on
humanitarian grounds with respect to refugees.

Could the UNHCR, the UNDP, and other donors do a better job at
financing development activities for refugees? Concentrating on internal management reforms, as the UNHCR has recently begun to do,
would increase the confidence donors have in that institution and be
an essential first step toward increased funding. The UNHCR would
also have to change its basic mandate faster than has happened to date.
At present, the UNHCR's Executive Committee seems to be moving
away from activities that could be called developmental.[28] It would also
require bilateral donors and recipient nations alike to change their
concepts of beneficiaries and their time horizons. The World Food
Program initiative mentioned earlier should be applauded, watched
carefully, and emulated by other donors in their own programs.

The NGOs have been active with refugees and displaced persons in
Sudan. To the extent their funding derives from donor governments—
and it does—they are caught in the same bind. A plus, however, is that
they have the option of seeking other sources of support, should they
find the government of Sudan more receptive to NGO activities than
it has lately demonstrated. At present, NGOs are leaving Sudan because
of harassment. A change in attitude on the part of the government could
induce much greater NGO participation in development activities for
refugees and nonrefugees alike.

In summary, change is overdue in a variety of institutions, Sudanese
and foreign, if their response capacity is to match the needs at hand.
An appropriate next step might be an 'ICARA III' to assess current
and future needs of refugees in countries such as Sudan and to determine how some of the most urgent changes can be achieved. In the

meantime, a greater appreciation is needed of just how dissonant the situation has become.

NOTES

1. John R. Rogge, *Too Many, Too Long: Sudan's Twenty-Year Refugee Dilemma* (Totowa, NJ: Rowman and Allanheld Publishers, 1985), p. 70.

2. United States Department of State, Bureau for Refugee Programs, "Draft World Refugee Report 1990," (Washington, DC), p. 24.

3. All statistics on the numbers of refugees and displaced persons come from personal conversations with a State Department refugee program officer, March 1990.

4. Rogge, p. 55.

5. "Draft World Refugee Report 1990," p. 24.

6. Rogge, p. 56.

7. Peter Feiden, Lynellyn Long, and Kathryn Stewart, "Khartoum Displaced Assessment and Recommendations," a report prepared for USAID-Sudan (Washington, DC), February 15, 1990, p. 1.

8. United States Agency for International Development, Bureau for Africa, "Sudan Development Yardsticks," (Washington, DC, undated), p. 2.

9. United States Agency for International Development, Bureau for Africa, "Sudan—Broad Based, Sustainable Rural Growth," (Washington, DC, undated), p. 2.

10. The World Bank, *World Development Report, 1989* (New York: Oxford University Press, 1989), p. 199.

11. *Ibid.*, p. 208.

12. Unnumbered table on Sudan's central government finance annexed to "Sudan Development Yardsticks."

13. United States Congress, Foreign Operations, Export Financing, and Related Programs Appropriations Act 1990, Public Law No. 101–167, Section 513, Volume 103, United States Statutes at Large, pp. 1195, 1219 (1989).

14. United States Congress, Foreign Operations, Export Financing, and Related Programs Appropriations Act 1990, Public Law No. 101–167, Section 518, Volume 103, United States Statutes at Large, pp. 1195, 1220 (1989).

15. United States Congress, Foreign Assistance Act of 1961, as amended, Section 617 (Title 22, United States Code, Section 2367).

16. United States Agency for International Development, "Congressional Presentation Fiscal Year, 1991" (Washington, DC), Annex 1, pp. 442–443.

17. United States Agency for International Development, Office of Financial Management, "Countries In or Near Violation of Section 620 (q) of the F.A.A. or the Brooke Amendment" (Washington, January 2, 1990).

18. United States Congress, Foreign Operations, Export Financing, and Related Program Appropriations Act 1990, Public Law No. 101–167, Section 572, Volume 103, United States Statutes at Large, pp. 1195, 1245 (1989).

19. Rogge, pp. 11–13.

20. Goran Melander and Peter Nobel, ed., *African Refugees and the Law* (New York: Africana Publishing Company, 1978), p. 13.

21. US Committee for Refugees, "Testimony of Roger P. Winter before House Select Committee on Hunger" (Washington, DC, February 8, 1990), p. 5.

22. W. R. Smyser, *Refugees: Extended Exile* (New York: Praeger for the Center for Strategic and International Studies, 1987), Washington Papers Series, pp. 70–71.

23. Rogge, p. 139.

24. Rogge, p. 176.

25. World Food Program, Committee on Food Aid Policies and Programs, "Review of Protracted Emergency Operations for Refugees and Displaced Persons," WFP/CFA/27/P/7 (Rome, April 19, 1989), pp. 14–15.

26. Rogge, p. 133.

27. *Ibid.*, p. 136.

28. Personal communication from a State Department refugee program officer, April 1990.

Farmers and the Failure of Agribusiness in Sudan

Stephen Kontos

Not more than a decade ago, Sudan was widely regarded as the future "breadbasket" of the Arab world, a vast, fertile land with abundant water from the Nile watershed. International lenders and oil-rich Arab investors poured more than $2 billion into Sudan's agricultural sector between 1975 and 1985, yet, during this period, its farm productivity stagnated and export earnings actually declined.[1] For a country in which 40 percent of the gross national product and more than 90 percent of its export revenues come from agriculture, such a failure is a bitter one indeed.

The failure of large-scale commercial agriculture in Sudan was evident even before the economic crisis, political instability, and natural disasters of the mid-1980s. Of all the major agricultural projects started in the 1970s and early 1980s, not one can be said to have been a commercial success.[2] Those still operating have done so at a loss, providing little, if any, return to their shareholders. Several—the $750 million Kenana Sugar Corporation estate, for example—are considered technically successful, but shortages of foreign exchange, poor transportation links, lack of skilled labor, and declining international commodity prices have made them dependent on subsidies for survival.

Most of the projects that failed did so because of economic or environmental problems. For many, the common denominator has been poor land. Because land in the vicinity of the Nile cannot be easily transferred or sold,[3] some of the largest farm projects, such as the 700,000 feddan Faisal Agricultural Corporation project, were established in remote areas on marginal land. Far from the Nile's fertile soil and dependent on erratic summer rains, these projects were handicapped from the start. Access to good soil and water for irrigation, in most cases, would have required the participation of local farmers, something that few organizations, public or private, have managed successfully. In Sudan, most projects that involved local farmers incurred heavy financial losses primarily because the farmers had little incentive to improve productivity. What is remarkable in Sudan, though, is that even the few projects that offered farmers sufficient incentives were commercial failures as well.

In this article, two examples of this phenomenon provide a useful measure of farmers' attitudes in Sudan's irrigated sector. One, a project in northern Sudan started in 1979 by Tenneco, a US multinational corporation, is a graphic example of local farmers failing in a major commercial venture. Despite incentives, which included a direct role in management and shares in the profits, the venture quickly fell apart because of the farmers' lack of commitment to their own cooperative. Their inability or reluctance to work toward the long-term objectives of the venture deprived them of long-term profits. Although they understood the rationale for the project and had already seen the benefits of the new technology introduced by the US sponsor, they had few expectations from it and even less confidence in its prospects for success. The second example is the 2.1 million feddan Gezira scheme, Sudan's largest irrigated estate. Farmers there showed a similar lack of commitment to the scheme's overall viability, notwithstanding better incentives offered by the Sudan Gezira Board (SGB) after 1980. In spite of favorable terms for cotton—Gezira's main cash crop—many farmers continued to divert their water and fertilizer rations to local market, fast return crops such as sorghum.

This seemingly self-defeating attitude is related to two major trends that have helped shape Sudan over the last 20 years. First has been the well-entrenched tendency toward government control of the economy, which climaxed in the 1970s with then-president Jaafar Numayri's nationalization of businesses, banks, and trade unions, as well as tighter control over agriculture and commerce. The second trend has been the steadily increasing rate of emigration from rural areas to Khartoum and to Arab countries.

Government efforts to micro-manage the economy have left farmers with a deep mistrust of all institutions, even of their own cooperatives, which had come to serve as instruments of state intervention. At the same time, the migration of many farmers away from their districts disrupted bonds of kinship and longstanding ties to the land. Because of a lack of commitment or sense of common purpose, those who replaced them have shown little interest in long-term improvements, not to mention innovations offered by outside investors. That these attitudes are so widespread suggests that commercial agricultural ventures in Sudan will not be viable for years to come. Economic reforms are a prerequisite for the nation's recovery, but even if introduced, it will take many years before their impact is noticeable in the fields.

The Gezira Model and Irrigated Agriculture

The decline in Sudanese agriculture can be traced to two shifts in government and investors' priorities. One shift took place gradually in the years after independence, with the government asserting steadily greater control over farming on irrigated lands, thereby reducing farmers' incentives. The second occurred as undeveloped rainfed lands came to be seen as a potential source of new wealth. Together, these shifts sapped the real strength of Sudan's agricultural economy, namely irrigated farming.

The conceptual ancestor of the big agricultural investments of the 1970s was the Gezira scheme established in 1911 by the Sudan Plantation Syndicate, a private British consortium.[4] Located on the rich alluvial plain between the White Nile and the Blue Nile, Gezira is ideal for irrigated production of a wide range of crops. Under the auspices of the syndicate—and, after independence in 1956, the SGB—the scheme was devoted to producing long-staple cotton for export to Britain and other overseas markets. It also became the home for 96,000 tenant farmers, many of whom had migrated from the northern provinces. The scheme had the main ingredients of commercial success: water, good soil, a stable labor base, and (at the time) a high-value crop with an assured market. Other government estates started after independence, such as the Rahad, New Halfa, and Agricultural Reform Corporation projects, followed the Gezira model of tenant farmers growing one or two major export crops under the management of a state-owned company. The more "successful" private projects of the 1970s were also irrigated and lay in the fertile areas adjoining the major rivers. Like the Gezira, these projects incorporated small farmers as tenants or sharecroppers.[5]

The importance of irrigated farms along the riverbanks is underlined by the fact that, even with all the investment in new areas, they still account for the bulk of Sudan's farm production and exports. For example, the Gezira scheme represented less than 11 percent of Sudan's cultivated area at the close of the 1970s, yet it alone produced 60 percent of the country's cotton, 75 percent of its wheat, and 35 percent of its groundnuts.[6] Irrigation enables farmers to take advantage of the cool (though rainless) winter in Sudan by planting temperate-zone crops such as wheat, fava beans, and many types of vegetables. In addition, control over water allows farmers to plant and harvest at optimum times, using up to three rotations a year. On the other hand, very little irrigated alluvial land is uninhabited and untended. As a result, individual farmers have—and will continue to have—a crucial role to play in the Sudanese economy. With the recurrence of drought in the region and the low productivity of the rainfed land, it is unlikely that this role will be diminished in the foreseeable future.

Rainfed Agriculture

Investments in the 1970s focused on the development of new areas, primarily rainfed lands to the east and south of Gezira. In contrast to Gezira and its counterparts, however, these projects—notably the large fully mechanized farms, such as the Faisal scheme—never lived up to expectations and certainly did not provide a viable alternative to irrigated estates. The quality of their soil was a major constraint—it was poor in nutrients and often high in salinity and mineral content. On the mechanized farms, yields of sorghum, a staple crop, averaged less than half those in the irrigated areas and below one-fifth those in developed countries.[7]

In Sudan, unless the soil is fertile, the expense of irrigation is prohibitive. Heavy use of fertilizers may improve crop performance enough to compensate for poor soil, but Sudanese farmers must import fertilizer, along with fuel, machinery, and other inputs. Given the high costs for these items, not to mention the scarcity of foreign exchange, the productivity of the rainfed lands is far too low to justify the use of fertilizer, much less major expenditures for equipment and farm infrastructure. Farm productivity is further hampered by outmoded cultivation practices and, unlike most other developing countries, an insufficient work force to support the labor intensive cultivation common on rainfed as well as irrigated farmland.[8] Another constraint on rainfed farming is the short growing season—three to six months—characterized by intense heat and unpredictable rainfall. The soil and climate severely limit the variety of crops that can be grown, which in turn increases the farmer's risk, whether from market fluctuations or crop failure. Only sorghum, sesame, short-fiber cotton, and some varieties of groundnuts are suited for large-scale cultivation in the rainfed areas, but, according to Food and Agriculture Organization figures, at least 80 percent of rainfed cropping is sorghum alone. The prevalence of a sorghum monoculture merely poses the additional risk of depleting the already poor soil quality.[9]

Given the poor outlook for rainfed farming, why were investors even tempted to shift their attention away from existing irrigated estates such as the Gezira? In large part, they did so because of the (paradoxically) disappointing performance of the irrigated estates, not to mention the perceived difficulty of managing the resident farmers on the land. As events in the 1970s and 1980s were to show, each of these problems fed the other.

Gezira's Failure

The large irrigated estates in Sudan, notably the Gezira scheme, resolved the issue of land and people by incorporating local farmers as tenants. Under the tenant system, the estate management (in most cases a government corporation) controls water, provides services and inputs, dictates what is to be produced, and markets the harvested crops.

The system is well suited to labor-intensive crop production, stable market conditions, and centralized management—essentially the environment of the 1920s rather than that of the 1980s. The hallmark of the Gezira tenant farming system has been its extensive control over the activities of the tenants. This is evident in the original basic tenancy agreements between SGB and each of its tenant farmers:

■ The tenant shall grow only cotton and sorghum, the latter for personal consumption only, not for sale. [Wheat and groundnuts were later added to the rotation.] All cotton shall be delivered to the SGB which will pay the farmer 40 percent of profits to be credited to a joint account.

■ The farmer must pay the SGB for water, fertilizer, mechanized farm operations [such as plowing and the application of pesticides] and other services provided by the Board. These charges are deducted from the joint account as a fixed percentage of the profits for the year.

■ The farmer is responsible for the irrigation of his plot, maintenance of feed canals, weeding, harvesting cotton [by hand], and clearing his fields of stubble left from previous crops.[10]

The joint account system, finally discontinued after the 1981–82 season after pressure from the World Bank, was the most obvious, but by no means the sole, disincentive for farmers. By charging percentages rather than fixed costs, the joint account system penalized the more productive farmers. Despite other measures to improve incentives, such as bonuses and price premiums, overall productivity in the Gezira project did not significantly improve during the 1980s. Evidently, more far-reaching changes were needed, as suggested in a 1987 US Department of Agriculture study:

Managers presently decide on cropping patterns and input use within large irrigated schemes like Gezira and Rahad, and tenants have minimal decision-making power and operate only within a restricted economic environment. The only major decisions that tenants control are timing of weeding and harvesting and allocation of labor between hired [workers] and family for various operations. Hence, while price incentives may have been initiated, tenants do not have the freedom to allocate their resources in response to the changing structure of incentives. This suggests that effects of macroeconomic policy reforms may not be as expected and a further understanding of pricing changes on the efficiency of resource allocation is necessary.[11]

In theory, as market conditions change for the worse, other crops would become more attractive to farmers, who would then seek ways to profit from the market regardless of management policy. In Gezira, limiting the cash crops to cotton threatened farmers' incomes when prices for cotton began to fall in the 1970s. Unless the SGB increased subsidies, which it was in no position to do, farmers stood to lose money by growing cotton. In fact, however, most farmers cheated on the system by illegally allocating resources to maximize the yields of other crops, especially sorghum.

Sorghum is a particularly attractive crop for Gezira farmers because, unlike cotton, groundnuts, or wheat, there is a free market for it throughout Sudan. Many farmers therefore give extra water to their sorghum at night, though the SGB specifically prohibits watering after dark. Another common practice is for farmers to obtain a fertilizer ration from the SGB for planting cotton and then use it for sorghum or even sell it on the black market. Other examples of tenants' resourcefulness in beating the SGB were noted by a British observer in 1980:

> ... Farmers [on the Gezira scheme] find many ways of manipulating or evading the regulations. ... Tenant absenteeism is widespread. Cotton may be transferred from tenant to tenant either in *shayl* (loan) transactions or to avoid debt repayment. Many tenants let out their land ... to sub-tenants on a sharecropping basis. Encroachment of livestock on cotton and other crops seems to have greatly increased. Labor-saving methods of crop watering are used instead of those officially prescribed.[12]

New incentives introduced in 1980 by the SGB had little effect and, if anything, made matters worse. The SGB offered immediate cash bonuses to farmers who obtained yields of over 3.5 kantars per feddan of long-staple cotton and above 5 kantars for medium-staple cotton. (One kantar equals 143 kilograms of seed cotton.) No sooner had these been introduced than a black market appeared in which tenants with surpluses sold cotton to less productive farmers who needed more to qualify for the bonus.[13]

Similar tenant systems exist on the other major parastatal schemes, including the Rahad, the Blue Nile Corporation, and Khasm al-Girba, all of which face comparable problems with productivity and farmer incentive. Although successful irrigated farming in Sudan will continue to depend on local farmers and laborers, the Gezira no longer suffices as a model for bringing farmers into large-scale commercial farming projects. The tenant system, therefore, will have to give way to a new model that better preserves the independence of individual farmers.

Investors considering agricultural projects in Sudan must take into account two related factors: first, that new projects on marginal land away from the Nile will probably not be cost-effective and, second, that use of the land near the river will require an accommodation with local farmers which avoids the inadequacies of the Gezira tenant system. Ideally, if there were a free economy, investors could purchase the land or develop it in joint ventures with local landowners. The Sudanese economy, however, is not free. Moreover, the privately-owned farmland still left near the river is fragmented into plots far too small to support economies of scale. A model tailored to the current political and demographic realities of Sudan, consequently, would lie somewhere between privately-owned estates and the government-owned corporations, more along the lines of farmers' cooperatives or partnerships. The problem in Sudan is that even these have failed to improve farm productivity.

Contract Farming

In the developed countries, one model that has successfully brought small farmers into commercial production and marketing schemes is contract farming. This model involves either seasonal or long-term contracts between individual farmers and corporations that process and market the crops. Unlike developed countries, however, to be successful in Sudan contract farming would require companies to help farmers complete the transition from subsistence to market-oriented farming.

They would need to modernize infrastructure and be directly involved in producing the crop, rather than merely marketing it. At the same time, they would have to preserve the incentives that motivate individual farmers.

At least one US multinational, Tenneco, did exactly this during the early 1980s, attempting to establish a contract farming venture with hundreds of local farmers who had organized their own cooperatives. Despite a conscious effort to preserve farmer incentives, the experiment failed completely. The incentives provided under the contracts were singularly effective in motivating the farmers, yet the results were disastrous, not just for the company but for the cooperatives and, ultimately, the farmers themselves.

In 1979, the company established a pilot farm in a remote area of the north. The original purpose of the project, which was called the Sahara Agricultural Venture (SAV), was to develop saline land in the desert and ultimately to use it for the export of fruit and vegetables to Saudi Arabia. After two years of operation, however, it became clear that the project would not be commercially viable. Faced with low productivity, along with the high cost of land reclamation, SAV's management devised an alternate strategy for the project. Because the pilot farm lay close to an extensive stretch of fertile, underused land adjoining the Nile, it was proposed that SAV provide technical assistance to local farmers, work with them to bring their land into full production, and market the crops. To do this, SAV opted for a system of contract farming based on a model conceived by Orville Freeman, former secretary of agriculture of the Kennedy and Johnson administrations, and Ruth Karen. As Freeman and Karen put it, both the farmers and the company would benefit from

> . . . harnessing the dynamic of the private sector, specifically by creating a symbiosis of corporate know-how, farmer devotion to the land and sound government policy. . . . . In agriculture, a private sector resolution of world problems means mobilizing smallholders . . . around a corporate core that effectively moves these farmers from subsistence agriculture into the market economy, as both producers and consumers, with all the developmental multiplier effects this implies, socially as well as economically.[14]

Practically speaking, SAV proposed to work with local cooperative societies, which had large enough tracts of land for mechanized farming—an average of 500 feddans each—as well as the necessary pumps, canals, and labor. Unlike Gezira and other tenant farming schemes, the cooperatives were owned and operated by local farmers and shareholders. As such, they offered an ideal combination of size, resources, and private incentives. Rather than assume the entire burden of managing and supervising hundreds of farmers, SAV intended to work jointly with the cooperative managers in carrying out the venture. The "corporate core" would comprise both the cooperative societies and SAV, thereby assuring the farmers that management would take their interests into account. With the organizational infrastructure thus established, SAV's staff would be able to devote themselves to the technical aspects of the venture, while minimizing the uncertainties of a foreign company working with local farmers.

The history of the local cooperative societies augured well for the success of the contract farming project, as they represented an example of home-grown initiative and self-sufficient rural development in Sudan. The Northern Province's first farmers' cooperative societies were formed in the 1930s, not far from the SAV site, by Sudanese who had worked in Egypt and had seen similar societies there.[15] Shareholders pooled cash and, in many instances, private land-holdings to create large farms extending into the empty government-owned land farther from the river. Share capital went toward leasing government land, as well as purchasing and installing mechanical pumps, while farmers contributed their labor to construct earthen dikes for the main irrigation canals. The societies were managed by a board elected by the farmers. The board made all decisions about expenditures, loans, and other matters, though, in practice, societies would often put major issues to a direct vote by the farmers. In addition, the boards would frequently hire or appoint a farm manager and a mechanic for maintenance of the pumps. The formula for distribution of the crops worked out by the early cooperative societies, and prevalent to this day, was a straight 50:50 division between the cooperative society and the farmers. The cooperative's 50 percent was expected to cover farm expenses such as fuel and parts for the pumps, seeds, fertilizer, and salaries for the manager and mechanic. Any surplus cash or crop production accruing to the cooperative was converted into dividends to be distributed to the shareholders. The farmers' 50 percent compensated them for their labor in plowing, planting, distributing water, weeding, harvesting, and threshing.

In effect, the cooperative societies mobilized the resources of their communities with the aim of utilizing up-to-date technology (at the time, mechanical pumps) and expanding cultivation. In the early years, the Anglo-Egyptian government encouraged this trend by offering land at low rents, but, unlike the Gezira scheme, the initiative came from the farmers themselves:

> The government schemes and the private schemes did not directly promote the cooperative movement, but directly created an atmosphere which the male landholders saw as an example for cooperative efforts to start similar pump schemes for increasing production.[16]

The formation of cooperative societies also provided an innovative solution to the problem of land fragmentation resulting from Islamic inheritance law. Under Islamic law, it is mandatory for property to be divided among all offspring (though not in equal shares for sons and daughters). Unless land is sold, it is not unusual to find a five-feddan field owned by scores of people, none of whom has a viable unit for farming. According to one study, Sudan, at one point, averaged 300 co-owners for every 10 feddans of private farmland in Northern Province.[17]

Largely because of the initiative of the cooperative societies, the area under cultivation in the north increased more than fourfold between 1935 and 1960. Cooperatives now account for about 40 percent of all registered farmland in Northern Province, while the remainder belongs to government-owned tenant estates (37 percent) or is freehold (23 percent).[18]

Failure of the SAV Experiment

By 1980 cooperative societies were but a shadow of what they had been before 1960. A SAV study, completed in 1980, determined that less than half the cooperative land remained under cultivation, while the societies themselves were financially incapable of maintaining their existing pumps and canals, much less of making new investments. In the vicinity of SAV, 11 active cooperatives, holding title to 6,655 feddans, saw the number of their farmers drop by almost half—from 1,000 to 550—between 1970 and 1980. By 1983, according to a SAV estimate, less than 30 percent of cooperative land was planted each year. SAV attributed the decline of the cooperatives primarily to Sudan's economic difficulties such as high production costs and low farm prices and the inability of cooperatives to modernize their production. The SAV management reasoned that, if the cooperatives could adopt modern production and marketing techniques, the decline could be reversed. SAV failed to consider, however, that no amount of technical assistance could restore the initiative that had driven the cooperatives in their early days.

SAV proposed to revitalize the cooperatives by introducing new irrigation techniques (by means of precision land leveling) and fully mechanizing their production.[19] As unused cooperative land was brought back into production, individual farmers could expect to farm much larger plots, while crop yields would improve and unit production costs would fall to competitive levels. To maintain an equitable sharing of costs (given that farm machinery owned or contracted by the cooperative societies would take over much of the farmers' manual labor), the cooperatives and the farmers needed to change their crop distribution ratio from 1:1 to 7:1—that is, rather than half for the cooperative and half for the farmers, the cooperative would receive seven-eighths and the farmers one-eighth.

Two farmers who worked on a 30-feddan plot leveled for demonstration purposes agreed that one of them could have handled twice the acreage under the new system. Assuming the cooperative societies mechanized their production, assigned farmers to larger plots, and made the corresponding changes in crop distribution, they would not only cover the costs of mechanization but also assure farmers of a higher income than under the old system. SAV calculated that one farmer working on a 60-feddan plot under the new distribution system would see at least a 700 percent increase in his income. The cooperative would earn at least a 20 percent profit after operating and capital costs, the latter mainly for land leveling. During a transitional period of up to five years, SAV offered to provide its farm machinery on a contract basis until the cooperatives could purchase their own, preferably through SAV. Similarly, SAV proposed to take responsibility for marketing the crops, thereby receiving a share of the profits from sales, particularly in export markets.

After demonstrating the benefits of the new system on the trial plot, SAV found that both the leaders and other members of the local cooperatives were enthusiastic about it, even with the change in crop distribution. The company subsequently signed contracts with four cooperatives for land leveling and mechanized services, contingent on their receiving loans from the Agricultural Bank of Sudan for the leveling; the question of marketing was deferred until more land was brought under production. The bank's management was similarly impressed with the idea and agreed to three of the four loans, although only one was processed in sufficient time to coincide with the crop season. Local and national government officials, as well as members of the surrounding communities, were excited about the initiative, believing that it might attract further investment by both Sudanese and foreigners. The government was determined to see the venture succeed, and it made every effort to ensure the timely delivery of fuel and fertilizer (both state-controlled commodities) despite severe shortages.

The cooperative that signed the first contract had only about 12 active farmers at the time because it had just resumed operations after a hiatus of nearly 20 years. By the next year, more farmers from the community, as well as others from the surrounding villages, had joined the cooperative. SAV's local staff estimated that the number of farmers would rise to more than a hundred because everyone who was a cooperative member (or his sons) had the privilege of working the land if he wanted to. Although the cooperative had 750 feddans—more than enough to go around—only 100 feddans had been leveled at that point. In membership meetings, the farmers nonetheless argued that everyone who wanted should be allowed to work on the leveled land, although that would have made for individual plots of one feddan or less, defeating the whole purpose of the venture. One counterproposal called for rotating several different farmers onto the leveled land each season, while letting the others cultivate the traditional way elsewhere on the farm but, the idea was rejected. Eventually leaders and members reached a compromise solution that would allow 30 farmers each to work approximately three feddans of leveled land. The farmers, however, soon pressed the cooperative leadership for additional changes that threatened to unravel the entire initiative.

The farmers argued that given the division of land, the seven-eighths versus one-eighth division of the crop was unfair. One-eighth from three feddans was indeed minuscule, so they proposed that distribution be changed back to 50:50. Some farmers again argued against any limitation on the number permitted to work the leveled land. In addition, one group demanded that they be allowed to use the traditional method of irrigation by using small pools of water (*hiyad*) on the leveled land. Not only would this have deprived other farmers of water unless they, too, used the hiyad, it would have made impossible the use of farm machinery. At the same time, bitter arguments erupted among the farmers over who should work the best plots of land, and none would accept the solution of rotating leveled plots among them. Despite the efforts of both the cooperative leaders and SAV staff, the farmers effectively stifled the entire program by voting to return to the 50:50 distribution of the crop. The remarkable part of the farmers' decision was that it put their own cooperative in a precarious financial situation, eventually forcing it to default on its loans and, of course, forego the profits that would have enabled it to expand.

The land leveling and mechanization concept itself was not an issue among the farmers. Although a few questioned its value, dozens of others with their own private plots (usually not more than 10 feddans and, therefore, not viable units for the program) offered to pay considerably more than the going rate for land leveling. The seven-eighths to one-eighth distribution of the crop was also not the main issue, as SAV had worked with farmers on this basis to grow wheat on its own land. Each farmer at SAV had been assigned 20 feddans, and, despite SAV's distance from their villages, most had returned for subsequent seasons. What then was the issue? It was clear from the actions and statements of the farmers that they had no confidence in the cooperative society and saw no benefit in working to enhance the welfare of the whole unit. Instead, each farmer sought to maximize his own return, even at the expense of the cooperative. The objective of the new program was to raise the productivity of the cooperative over a period of several years, but, rather than commit themselves to such a distant goal, most of the farmers preferred to concentrate on the short term and get what they could, while they could. That they held shares in the cooperative and would be entitled to share its profits did not, evidently, weigh heavily in their thinking.

Farmers and the State

The attitudes of the Gezira farmers and their counterparts in the Northern Province cooperative societies have much in common. The SGB and the cooperatives, over time, completely lost the confidence of farmers. Farmers no longer believe that either institution effectively preserves or promotes their interests. At best, the SGB and cooperative societies are considered ineffectual. At worst, they are regarded (like the Sudanese government itself) as adversaries who undercut the efforts of the individual farmer. Similarly, farmers have little faith in the management of these institutions, an attitude that hinders efforts to introduce new technology and farming methods. The evidence for this malaise lies, first, in the unusually low productivity of these farms and, second, in the large number of farmers or tenants who have left them.

Under the Numayri government, the cooperatives began to take on more of the character of parastatal farms such as the Gezira. The 1973 Cooperative Act (amended in 1977) all but nationalized cooperative societies, placing them under the direct control of the state. The general provisions of the act refer to the "right of the State to supervise the Cooperative Movement and to guide it towards its objectives."[20] Besides limiting the scope of the cooperatives' business transactions, such as distributing profits, taking out loans, and selling shares, the Cooperative Act required that members defer to the new Ministry of Cooperation in questions of management. To administer the act, the government assigned local officials to participate in membership meetings and advise the cooperative boards. Along with increased government supervision, the act mandated subsidies for seeds, fertilizer, pesticides, and other farm inputs, as well as assuring the cooperatives of priority for government services, the most important being allocations of petroleum products. Cooperatives were exempt from taxes on "commercial and industrial profits," but 10 percent of their "surplus" income was to be contributed to "local development, support for the Cooperative Movement, training [and] cooperative education and social services for its members . . . "[21]

In addition, the minister of cooperation had broad powers to determine the use of all surplus funds, appoint members to the boards, and set guidelines for contracts and borrowing funds. The act was consistent with Numayri's efforts to impose central government control over a variety of institutions, ranging from banks to trade unions. Companies, cooperatives, unions, and, of course, political parties were regarded as rival bases of power, hence Numayri tightened his grip on them through legislation and, in the cases of many private firms, outright confiscation. Private companies that were not nationalized suffered through the selective allocation of state-controlled services and commodities, notably fuel, fertilizer, and credit.

Under these circumstances, farmers quickly lost confidence in the cooperative societies. Thousands of young men emigrated from the north during this period.[22] Others continued to farm, but abandoned membership in cooperatives to lease their own small plots on land farther out in the desert; water for these plots came from shallow bore wells. The regional government, short of cash, was more than willing to award leases to anyone prepared to pay both a title fee and annual rent for desert land. Despite the poor quality of the soil, many farmers preferred this land to remaining on that of the cooperatives. Savings and remittances from emigrants went increasingly to pay for their relatives' small wells and pump sets rather than to develop cooperatives. When SAV started its contract farming program, farmers on small plots besieged the company with requests for land leveling and other services. It is hard to imagine a more inefficient use of resources and capital than this. While thousands of feddans of prime farmland lay idle, individual farmers committed their money and energy to postage stamp-sized farms that could not pay for themselves in the foreseeable future.

Farmers who remained on the cooperatives did so with the least of expectations. Under the 1973 Cooperative Act, they found that a major benefit of cooperative membership was the privilege of obtaining seeds, fertilizer, and other inputs at subsidized prices and doing so with priority over private farmers. At the same time, cooperative farmers came to believe that the government would prop up financially strapped cooperatives in the same way that it did for the parastatal farms. Whether for this reason or because of government levies on surplus cooperative funds, it became the norm for cooperative societies to operate at a deficit or, at best, not to record profits on their books. Farmers had every reason to conceal harvested crops from the cooperative and to understate the produce from their plots.[23] They were also less inclined to devote their time to work on behalf of the cooperative. Over time, maintenance of the canals and pumps was neglected, and cooperative infrastructure deteriorated. A 1980 SAV survey of 15 cooperatives revealed that none had posted any profits during the previous five years and that most of their canals and pumps were either unusable or in serious disrepair.[24] Most cooperative farmers were interested merely in producing crops for subsistence, and so their horizons seldom extended beyond one or two crop seasons. Cash cropping was done elsewhere, usually on private plots or in household gardens. Farmers were also quick to leave the cooperatives if the work became too demanding or if production suffered for any reason such as pump breakdowns or collapse of canal banks. They might move on to another cooperative, emigrate from the area entirely, or, if they had enough savings, lease their own plots in the desert. Unlike the decades before the 1970s, they rarely opted to remain with the cooperative and to invest their labor and capital in repairs and improvements. As a result of this new mobility, farmers had little sense of responsibility to the cooperative society, much less an interest in innovations or long-term development.

The Gezira scheme has suffered from a similar lack of confidence among its tenants. Tenants have little say in what they grow or how they grow it. As market prices for cotton have declined, they have lost the incentive to do anything but grow crops for subsistence. More often tenants have quit the scheme entirely, leaving their tenancies to be farmed by sharecroppers or hired laborers. (Tenants cannot legally sell or lease their rights to the land.) SGB figures indicate that fewer than half of all tenants are still directly involved in farming, and only 15 percent of the overall labor requirements are met by tenants and their families. It is safe to say that the majority of work on the Gezira scheme is done by migrant workers, primarily from western Sudan. In 1983, according to the World Bank, 56 percent of the work force consisted of migrant laborers, and 29 percent were resident hired laborers.[25]

Kinship and Agriculture

For Gezira, as for the cooperative societies, demographic changes have had a subtle but profound effect on farm productivity. As established farmers (or tenants) departed in search of better opportunities and were replaced by sharecroppers and migrant laborers or by farmers from outside the community, both family and community ties have been weakened. Until the mid-twentieth century, the basic economic and social unit in the riverain areas of northern Sudan has been the *sagiya*, which combined the labor of each extended family to cultivate an irrigated plot. The sagiya, literally, was the wooden ox-driven water wheel normally used to irrigate several feddans. In the vocabulary of the northern Sudanese, it also refers to an extended family group, which "was an independent unit in making its own decisions concerning crops, areas to be cultivated, crop rotations."[26] El-Haj Bilal Omer, a Sudanese sociologist, in his book about social changes in Northern Province, observed that a significant decline has occurred in the "corporateness and solidarity of the extended family, which has gradually given way to a nuclear family organization."[27] He argues that, as large-scale farming in the north has replaced the sagiya system of farming, extended family ties have been diluted. At the same time, "Cooperation in the production process [is] decreasing," since individuals are more self-sufficient, relying more and more on technology, not to mention other opportunities, such as wage labor.[28] Unfortunately, no credible institutions have emerged to replace the sagiya as a focus of individual loyalties and confidence.[29] In the past, cooperatives consisted primarily of farmers from a single village, most of whom had extended family relationships. Nowadays, village and family ties are still important elements of a person's identity in northern Sudan, but they are less likely to be combined with membership in a cooperative. Hence, as cooperatives replaced their original members with farmers from other villages (or even from other provinces), the thread of common identity and purpose was broken and cooperative organization began to disintegrate.

Because so many Gezira tenants are of northern Sudanese origin, the sagiya system of extended family cooperation was, in the past, important for meeting the labor needs of each 10-feddan tenancy. As in Northern Province, the migration of family members away from the Gezira scheme increased reliance on outside labor. Although the influence of tenants on SGB policy is limited, this demographic shift nonetheless widened the gap between them and the management. The importance of sorghum as payment in kind to migrant laborers illustrates this. Sorghum functions as a sort of currency in central Sudan and is widely marketable, so it is the payment of choice for outside laborers. As the demand for migrant labor has increased, tenants' and laborers' resistance to SGB curbs on growing sorghum has intensified.[30] The reliance on outside labor is now so widespread in the Gezira that the current tenant system has become outmoded and actually hinders productivity. Many tenants are no more than middlemen, living in towns and doing the minimum necessary to retain their rights to the land. Growing sorghum, by no means the most profitable crop in Sudan, at least allows them to pay laborers and have a marketable crop as well. Until the SGB allows tenants to lease or sell their rights to the land, this sort of attitude will persist and continue to hold back productivity.

Farmers, Productivity, and Progress

Throughout Sudan's irrigated sector, the trend during the 1970s and early 1980s was toward greater government control and centralization. Changing conditions in the world market merely accentuated the rigidities and disincentives of centralized farm management in Sudan. For the most part, foreign assistance programs encouraged a greater government role in agriculture insofar as they placed considerable amounts of foreign exchange and imported goods at the disposition of the central government. Also, exports of cotton and several other agricultural commodities were among the few sources of foreign exchange that accrued directly to the central treasury.

With these benefits, not to mention the huge bureaucracies spawned by government agricultural activities, it is unlikely that conditions for small farmers will change significantly in the near future. Successive governments in Sudan have apparently convinced themselves that "job security" and government supports, in the form of subsidies and services, will satisfy farmers' aspirations, but centrally managed agriculture in Sudan must confront the same questions as the private schemes: is it possible to compensate farmers adequately for their loss of decision-making power and control over their land and crops?

Orville Freeman's concept of contract farming through a "corporate core" attempted to resolve this problem while introducing modern economies of scale. Because such initiatives depend on capital and technical expertise—crucial in Sudan, given the complexity of irrigated farming—it often necessitates a delicate balance between a large organization such as a corporation, cooperative, or government agency on the one hand and the farmer and landholder on the other. The early Sudanese cooperative societies enabled small farmers themselves to strike this balance as well as to preserve it for many years. Only in the late 1960s and the 1970s did a combination of demographic changes and government intervention weaken the cooperatives to the point that they could barely provide subsistence for their members.

The irrigated sector in Sudan will continue to depend heavily on small farmers, hence it follows that the model of the pre-1973 cooperative societies is a good one for investors. Arthur Gaitskill, a British historian and authority on Gezira, alluded to this model in his 1959 book. In his list of recommendations, "Some Cardinal Principles, Supported by the Gezira Experience, Important to the Success of Development Projects of this Nature," he hinted that Gezira itself would be better off if it were turned over to cooperatives. New projects should be started, he argued, " . . . [with] an ultimate intention to withdraw the government partner and leave the undertaking to a cooperative, and [with] adequate preparation for that objective.''[31] The lesson of the SAV experience, however, is that Sudanese cooperative societies, as presently constituted and regulated, are far removed from their dynamic forerunners. Under the present system in the irrigated sector, farmers have no faith that their collective efforts will be rewarded. From the investor's perspective, tax holidays and other concessions under Sudan's investment code, however generous, will not offset the lack of motivation common among farmers and bureaucrats alike.

It appears unlikely that private investors or donor agencies will consider backing major new agricultural projects in Sudan, even if the political climate improves. Neither economic conditions nor the state of Sudan's own private sector give much reason for optimism. In any event, the key to reviving Sudan's commercial agriculture will not be so much an infusion of fresh capital as the creation of an environment that will promote its effective use. This means that private institutions, such as companies and cooperative societies, should operate free of government influence over their management. It means that they must make their own decisions about production, crop selection, marketing, use of profits, and—most of all—the sale or leasing of land. Finally, it means that farmers must themselves adapt to changes already in motion, such as technological advances, rapid shifts in world commodity markets, and the weakening of family and community ties. If past experience has shown anything, though, it is that the government should follow the lead of the farmers rather than expect farmers to follow that of the government. The future health of Sudan depends on them.

NOTES

1. Between 1974 and 1981, the period when most projects became operational, the annual volume of three major exports—cotton, groundnuts, and sesame—fell from an average of 168,000 tons, 99,000 tons, and 70,000 tons to 81,000 tons, 43,000 tons and 41,000 tons, respectively. World Bank, *Sudan: Investing for Economic Stabilization and Structural Change* (Washington, DC:

World Bank, 1982), Report No. 3551a-SU. For annual production figures of the major crops during this period, see Brian D'Silva, *Sudan: Policy Reforms and Prospects for Agricultural Recovery After the Drought* (Washington, DC: US Department of Agriculture, 1985).

2. Major foreign investments in agriculture during the 1970s included the Kenana Sugar Corporation, the Arab Sudanese Blue Nile Company, the Faisal Agricultural Corporation, the Tenneco Sahara Agricultural Venture, the Seleit Food Company, the Egyptian-Sudanese Integrated Company, Damazine Corporation, along with the Suki, Junaid, and Haggar al-Salaya sugar projects. The Triad Corporation of Adnan Khashoggi had rights for 500,000 feddans of undeveloped land, and 250,000 feddans were committed to Tenneco Inc. of Houston, but neither company used the land. (A feddan equals 1.038 acres.)

3. As the Anglo-Egyptian Condominium extended its rule over Sudan in the early 1900s, it divided all land into *milik* (private land) and *miyri* (government land). Any family that could prove that it had inhabited and farmed a particular plot of land received a deed formalizing its ownership. Any land that was unclaimed, or for which a claim could not be substantiated, reverted to government ownership. This, of course, meant that the bulk of the land in Sudan was under government control and remains so to this day. Conditions for leasing land are strict and forbid individuals to sell or transfer their rights (though, under current law, heirs have the right to renew a lease). The tiny amount of milik is subject to fewer restrictions under civil law, but Islamic inheritance law has led to the fragmentation of holdings and a near complete paralysis in transactions.

4. The original acreage of Gezira was 1.2 million feddans irrigated from water stored behind the Sennar Dam on the Blue Nile. The completion of the Roseires Dam allowed the addition of nearly 1 million feddans of adjacent land known as the Managil extension. See Arthur Gaitskill, *Gezira: A Story of Development in the Sudan* (London: Faber & Faber, 1959).

5. Some notable examples are the Arab-Sudanese Fruit and Vegetable Company, the Seleit Food Company, and the Abu Nama estate of the Sarkis Ismerlian Company.

6. World Bank, *Sudan*. See also D'Silva, *Sudan: Policy Reforms*, p. 16.

7. Food and Agriculture Organization, *Production Yearbook*, (Rome: FAO, 1986).

8. Even most of the "mechanized" farms in the rainfed areas depend on legions of migrant workers to harvest sorghum and sesame. The common varieties of Sudanese sorghum are not combinable, so laborers must cut the grain stalks and feed them by hand into combines for threshing. Sesame harvesting must also be done by hand, otherwise the seeds will shatter. The heavy dependence on manual labor increases costs, especially during bountiful crop seasons when competition for workers is keen. Efforts to introduce combinable sorghum hybrids and varieties to rainfed areas failed according to a study commissioned by Arkel International on behalf of the US Agency for Inter-

national Development. See also Morag C. Simpson, "Large-Scale Mechanized Rainfed Farming Developments in the Sudan" in *Post-Independence Sudan*, Proceedings from the seminar "Post-Independence Sudan," Centre of African Studies, University of Edinburgh, November 21–22, 1980, pp. 197–212.

9. Harold D. Nelson, ed., *Sudan: A Country Study* (Washington, DC: US Government Printing Office, 1983 [The American University Area Handbook Series]), p. 158. As early as 1975, a joint International Labor Organization and United Nations Development Programme team raised concerns about the rapid depletion of land in the rainfed areas. See International Labor Organization, *Growth, Employment and Equity: A Comprehensive Strategy for the Sudan* (Geneva: International Labor Organization, 1976), p. 47.

10. Gaitskill, *Gezira*, appendices.

11. Regarding the joint account system, see Brian D'Silva and Kamil Hassan, *Institutional Change, Incentive Effects and Choice of Technology in Sudan's Irrigated Subsector: A Model of the Rahad Scheme* (Washington, DC: US Department of Agriculture, 1987), p. 8; D'Silva, *Sudan: Policy Reforms*, p. 35.

12. I. G. Simpson, "Institutional Constraints to Agricultural Development in the Sudan" in *Post-Independence Sudan*, p. 157. See also D'Silva, *Sudan: Policy Reforms*, pp. 35–36 and D'Silva and Hassan, *Institutional Change*, pp. 9–10. In the latter report, D'Silva mentions that the management of the state-owned Rahad scheme mixed herbicides into the fertilizer to keep farmers from using it on sorghum. One can only guess the results of this misguided policy. Apart from wasting foreign exchange, any mistakes in labeling or storing the fertilizer could have led to the destruction of legitimate crops.

13. I. G. Simpson, "Institutional Constraints," p. 159.

14. Orville Freeman and Ruth Karen, *The Farmer and the Money Economy: The Role of the Private Sector in the Agricultural Development of LDC's* (New York: Business International Corporation, 1981), p. 15.

15. The first society was founded in 1934 at Mushu, a village on the Nile, about 10 miles from the SAV pilot farm. Under the commercial code at the time, the societies were private "trading companies" owned by shareholders. Many still retain the "Trading Company" designation in their charters.

16. W. S. Mann, *The Cooperative Movement in the Democratic Republic of the Sudan* (Khartoum: Khartoum University Press, 1978), p. 13.

17. Mohammed Hashim Awad, "The Evolution of Land Ownership in the Sudan," *Middle East Journal*, vol. 25, no. 3 (Spring 1971), pp. 212–28.

18. Figures from Ministry of Agriculture, Northern Province. In 1982, cooperatives accounted for 77,554 feddans out of the total of 195,718 feddans of registered farmland. A significant amount of cooperative acreage has been abandoned since the 1960s, however, figures are not readily available. Some observers estimate that the abandoned land represents at least half the total acreage.

19. The most labor-intensive part of Sudan's irrigated farming, especially

in Northern Province, is the system of water distribution. Virtually all farmers irrigate their fields with *hiyad* (small pools or basins). A field of only a few acres may contain dozens of these small hand-made basins, hence building and maintaining the hiyad takes up a substantial part of the farmer's time. The hiyad system not only restricts the area each farmer can cultivate, it makes mechanized cultivation and harvesting nearly impossible. SAV proposed using furrows or large basins extending up to several hundred yards without a break, something relatively easy to do since the introduction of laser-calibrated land leveling in the 1970s. This simplified water distribution and allowed easy access by farm machinery.

20. Democratic Republic of the Sudan, Council of Ministers, Cooperation Act of 1973, General Provisions; and Ministry of Cooperation, Commerce and Supply Cooperative Societies Bill, 1977 (in Arabic).

21. Cooperation Act of 1973, Article 39, paragraph iv.

22. Migration has long been a part of Nubian life, but in the last two decades, the flow of migrants has turned into a flood. A European Community (EC) report issued in 1980 states that, between 1956 and 1973, about 35 percent of the male population left the province to work in other parts of Sudan or in Arab countries. No formal estimates exist for later years, but it is commonly believed that the figure is now more than 50 percent. See European Community, "Northern Provinces Micro-Project Programme." See also Sir M. McDonald & Partners, Ltd. (Cambridge, UK), "Reappraisal of the Northern and Nile Provinces Pump Schemes," (Prepared for the Democratic Republic of the Sudan, Ministry of National Planning, Khartoum, 1979), pp. 47–48.

23. Growing conditions for temperate crops, such as wheat, in Northern Province are better than those in Gezira, yet posted yields are not appreciably different. Government statistics show average wheat yields in Northern Province at about 1.5 metric tons per hectare versus 1 ton in Gezira. Egypt, which has climatic and soil conditions comparable to those in Northern Province, has average wheat yields of more than 4 tons per hectare. Under-reporting of harvests in Northern Province is certainly one reason for the abnormally low figures. Another factor is the increased use of marginal desert land for private plots.

24. Two of the four cooperatives slated for the SAV land leveling program were selected largely because they had installed new pump sets bought with grants from the EC. The two others were located in areas of Northern Province with high per capita incomes. This wealth, it was hoped, could be tapped to pay for much needed maintenance of pumps and canals.

25. Interview with World Bank official.

26. El-Haj Bilal Omer, *The Danagla Traders of Northern Sudan: Rural Capitalism and Agricultural Development* (London: Ithaca Press, 1985), p. 6.

27. *Ibid.*, p. 29. Omer's thesis follows a Marxist paradigm, emphasizing that economic changes are prior to social changes: "The fact that the organi-

zation of economic production defines, in many respects, the kinship system and internal organization of the peasant families is an important proposition of this study." (Cf. p. 29.) This view belittles the role of kinship in preserving mutual confidence among participants in cooperative economic ventures.

28. *Ibid.*

29. See Brian D'Silva, *Sudan's Irrigated Subsector: Issues for Policy Analysis* (Washington, DC: US Department of Agriculture, 1986), p. 13.

30. This reflects continuation and intensification of the decline of the sagiya system that had begun already in the mid-nineteenth century. See Anders Bjørkelo, *Prelude to the Mahdiyya: Peasants and Traders in the Shendi Region: 1821–1885* (Cambridge and New York: Cambridge University Press, 1989), especially chapter 4.

31. Gaitskill, *Gezira*, Appendix III, p. 355.

Contributors

Bodour Abu Afan is the director of the Economic and Social Research Council in Khartoum and author of *Industrial Policies and Industrialization in the Sudan*.

Peter K. Bechtold is chair for Near East and African studies at the Foreign Service Institute and author of *Politics in the Sudan*. (The views expressed in his chapter do not necessarily represent the views of the US government.)

Francis Mading Deng is senior fellow in foreign policy studies at the Brookings Institution. He has served as Sudan's ambassador to Scandinavia (1972–1974), the United States (1974–1976), and Canada (1980–1983). He was minister of state for foreign affairs from 1976 to 1980. He is also the author of a number of anthropological studies and novels.

Carolyn Fluehr-Lobban is professor of anthropology at Rhode Island College, has served two terms as president of the Sudan Studies Association, and is the author of *Islamic Law and Society in the Sudan*.

Mary C. Kilgour is a senior foreign service officer with the Agency for International Development. (The views expressed in her chapter do not necessarily reflect those of the US government.)

Stephen Kontos is a US foreign service officer and a former representative of Tenneco in Sudan (1982–1986). (The views expressed in his chapter do not necessarily reflect those of the US government.)

Ann Mosely Lesch teaches Middle East politics at Villanova University and has written on Sudanese and Palestinian affairs. Her most recent book, co-authored with Mark Tessler, is *Israel, Egypt, and the Palestinians: From Camp David to Intifada.*

John O. Voll is professor of history at the University of New Hampshire and, along with Sarah P. Voll, is the author of *The Sudan: Unity and Diversity in a Multicultural State.*

Gabriel R. Warburg is professor of Middle Eastern history at the University of Haifa and the editor of *Asian and African Studies.* He is the author of *Islam, Nationalism, and Communism in a Traditional Society: The Case of Sudan.*

Index

Abbud, Ibrahim: military coup, 80; fall of regime, 90–91
Abdullah, Osman: TMC and Libya, 56
Abu Qurun, Nayal: sharia, 93–94, 106n
Addis Ababa agreement (1972): regional autonomy in south, 22n, 25; negotiation and terms, 80–81; relations between north and south, 99
Africa Watch: human rights abuses, 85
Africans: socio-cultural aspects of foreign policy, 45. *See also* South
Agriculture: role in economy, x; potential of, 2; decline in production and exports, 108–109, 137, 157n; export crops and stabilization program, 114, 118; rural settlement schemes for refugees, 125–26; land availability, 137–38; failure of commercial ventures, 138; rainfed, 140–41; contract farming, 144–51; farmers and the state, 151–54; kinship systems, 154–55; farmers, productivity, and progress, 155–57; foreign investment, 158n. *See also* Economics; Gezira scheme; Irrigation
Albino, Oliver: southern distrust of north, 75
Anglo-Egyptian Condominium government: conservatism of northern society, 35; administrative policies in north and south, 77; land policy, 158n
Ansar: Numayri's Islamic path, 92–93; as obstacle to democracy, 98; southern distrust, 100; Sadiq as prime minister, 103
Anti-Slavery Society: Islam and slave trade, 72, 73
Anya-Nya: federal constitution, 25
Arabization: government policies in south, 29–30
Arabs: identity of north, 26; language, culture, race, and Islam, 40n; socio-cultural aspects of foreign policy, 45. *See also* North
Authoritarianism: political culture and new politics, 21. *See also* Islamization
Awad al-Jid Ahmad: Numayri and sharia, 93–94, 106n
al-Azhari, Ismail: political transitions following independence, 3; call for Islamic state, 80

al-Bashir, Umar Hassan: schools of thought on staying power, 2; political transitions and tasks facing regime, 5–6; military coup, 16; pro-NIF policies, 16; civil service purges, 17–18; political participation, 18; response to opposition, 20; suppression of communism, 35; foreign policy, 63–67, 68; coup and sharia, 105. *See also* Revolutionary Command Council of National Salvation (RCC-NS)
British colonial government: image in south, 30; undermining of traditional African culture, 36; slave trade, 72, 74; administrative policies in north and south, 77–78; nationalist movements, 78–79
Brooke-Alexander amendment: U.S. and foreign aid, 127–28
Bush, George: U.S. relations with Numayri regime, 51
Buxton, Sir Thomas: Islam and slave trade, 73

Chad: TMC and Libya, 56; conflict with Libya and Bashir regime, 65–66; refugees, 125
Chevron: oil development and civil war, 11, 48–49, 51
Christianity: religious identities and value systems in south, 29